NEXT JOB,
BEST JOB

NEXT JOB, BEST JOB

A Headhunter's 11 Strategies to Get Hired Now

ROB BARNETT

CITADEL PRESS
Kensington Publishing Corp.
www.kensingtonbooks.com

CITADEL PRESS BOOKS are published by

Kensington Publishing Corp.
119 West 40th Street
New York, NY 10018

All Kensington titles, imprints, and distributed lines are available at special quantity discounts for bulk purchases for sales promotions, premiums, fund-raising, educational, or institutional use.

Special book excerpts or customized printings can also be created to fit specific needs. For details, write or phone the office of the Kensington sales manager: Kensington Publishing Corp., 119 West 40th Street, New York, NY 10018, attn: Sales Department; phone 1-800-221-2647.

CITADEL PRESS and the Citadel logo are Reg. U.S. Pat. & TM Off.

ISBN-13: 978-0-8065-4148-8
ISBN-10: 0-8065-4148-2

First printing: July 2021

10 9 8 7 6 5 4 3 2 1

Printed in the United States of America

Library of Congress Cataloging in Publication Number: 2021936513

Electronic edition:

ISBN-13: 978-0-8065-4150-1 (e-book)
ISBN-10: 0-8065-4150-4 (e-book)

To Janie, Sydney, Ukie, Stanley, Barbara, Irwin, Jeff, Kay, Doug, Suzanne, Sue, Julia, Sara, Jessie, and Dylan.

Contents

NEXT JOB,
BEST JOB

Introduction

Grandma Janie was a goddess of unconditional love in my life. Her spirit wants to share five words if you're struggling looking for work—a phrase she repeated anytime I was wrestling with a decision: "You'll know when you know."

After more than forty years in the work world, I finally know how to help people who are stuck in between jobs. If you're out of work right now, waiting too long to find the right answers, the right people, and your next, best job, this book will help turn pain into purpose to create what you need and deserve. Once your heart and head are firmly fixed on exactly what you're supposed to do next, the stress and pain of your job search will be replaced with strength and confidence that would make Janie proud.

If you're currently working but frustrated with your situation, or fearing you could get the boot any moment, the negative associations with two dirty words, *job search*, can bang like a war drum in your head. Searching for your next job does not need to be harder than winning the lottery. Instead of tossing your résumé into that mysterious hole filled with thousands of résumés, you can employ a new set of strategies that lead you into work that fits you better than anything you've done before.

On June 1, 2018, I'd been out of work for over six months. Every time I thought I was close to finally winning a new job, the decision maker came back with news that they were "going in another direction." I was frustrated, angry, sad, scared, and confused. I couldn't figure out what I was doing wrong and what it would take to get hired. Then, one day, I woke up with a powerful realization that it was time to shift focus. I made an instantaneous decision to turn all my energy, passion, and experience in a new direction. North.

At 9:00 a.m. on that life-changing summer morning, I grabbed my iPhone, turned on the video camera, and pressed record. One second before the first word came out of my mouth, I realized that I hadn't shaved, I was wearing a crappy old shirt, the lighting wasn't good, and there was a bunch of junk all over my room. But I went for it anyway.

I spoke briefly about my career in radio, television, film, online video, and podcasting. I had been a senior executive in major media companies and a digital entrepreneur. It was an amazing run so far. But I was stuck, badly. There were mouths to feed and miles to go before I could imagine taking my foot off the gas. I didn't want to bitch and moan about being unemployed, but I definitely wanted to set a tone of solidarity. Too many of my closest friends and longtime workmates were all in a similar state of trouble. I decided to name my unwelcome circumstance #iBJA (in between jobs, again).

I invited anyone interested in talking and thinking about this common problem to connect. I thought one of the keys to finding work could be tribal: "We can't do this as individuals as successfully as we can by doing it together . . . to help each other find the next, best projects." I promised to spend at least a few minutes each day talking about it. I ended Video #1 (called "From There to Here") by suggesting the start of a "new religion" called #JustRespond.

I uploaded the video before letting any thoughts about recording another take sink in. I posted it on LinkedIn and on my personal Facebook page. "Likes" started coming in fast. Comments began flying in and reactions were building more than any personal post I'd made in a long time. By the time night fell, there were over 16,000 views and about 600 comments. I'd struck a nerve. Most of the people said I echoed exactly what they were going through, secretly, on the inside. My phone was on fire with incoming calls, texts, and emails.

The next day, I put on a slightly nicer shirt and shaved. That morning (and every morning since), I upload one new short video—staying on the theme of getting as many of us back to work, as quickly as possible. After the first week of videos, and a constant flow of supportive responses, I heard from a man who said he was watching every morning. We met many years earlier, when I was working at MTV. He was running his own business now and was looking to hire a chief operating officer. He asked a question that changed my life, "Are you a headhunter?"

Without one second of hesitation, I said, "Yes!" Then I muted the call and started furiously typing into a Google search: *headhunter, recruiter, retainer, percentage . . .*

By the time he was ready to ask for the details on how my business worked, I was ready too. With total confidence in my voice, as if I had done this for years, I said that my standard deal included a percentage of the new employee's first-year salary. We talked more about the scope of the role and the responsibilities, the range of the total compensation package, and his best-case scenario for a timeline to fill the open job. I heard his confidence building as our conversation flowed and then he ended with this: "Let's do it."

I hung up and felt a rush of adrenaline. I called my lawyer to ask for a headhunter agreement to be written up at lightning speed.

A few minutes after this mind-altering call, I realized I was handed a career choice that never occurred to me for a nanosecond in the past. The single word *headhunter* became a new organizing principle in my mind. I found a mission. I would use five decades of executive experience to start a headhunting business and give people the inspiration, sharper tools, and a powerful plan to rewire their careers and win their next, best job.

All of our collective frustrations, angst, and fears about the hiring process is a disease I wanted to cure. My own past experiences as a job candidate left me craving more responsiveness, respect, transparency, and faster results. I decided to shift all my attention to finding new ways to solve these painful problems for as many people as possible. My daily video posts on every social media platform earned millions of views and gave birth to a living, breathing tribe for thousands of professionals. All of us are ready to replace the disrespect and non-responsiveness of the job search process with new methods that actually work.

Years of guiding people at every step of the hiring process built the strategies in this book to help your job search succeed with more speed and purpose. **There are now over 1000 episodes of my daily video series on RobBarnettMedia.com and on all of the social media channels to give job seekers free, daily advice and inspiration to put new search strategies to work.** If you're out of work and feeling lost at sea, you're holding a life preserver that can help you get to dry land, now. If you're currently working but secretly dying to get "out," or worried you'll be forced out soon, you're going to learn how to find a better job—a job you love. A special note to my unemployed readers: The agony of losing your job is a temporary pain that will heal and make room for renewed strength, a lighter heart, a quicker pace, a better sense of humor, and a megaton of new wisdom. You're going to graduate from the school of hard knocks into a new situation that's better suited for who you are and the work you want to do. You're going to work for a better boss, on a team with a clear mission. You're going to be given achievable goals, room to succeed, help when you need it, and rewards for your success. You're going to work for people who treat you the way you expect to be treated. You're going to work hard, but you're not going to work yourself to death. You're going to be smarter, more focused, and better organized.

I'm going to give you eleven new prescriptions. Be warned about the side effects of this treatment. You may experience:

- A focused game plan

- A sudden increase in confidence

- A new sense of purpose

- Mental clarity

- Renewed physical strength

- Constant itching to get back in the game

- A daily dose of empathy

- A positive new daily routine

- More restful sleep

- A passionate desire to stay focused

- Increased hunger to win

There are a few reasons this book is built on 11 strategies. I'm a huge fan of *This Is Spinal Tap*. If this reference doesn't immediately produce joy, you're missing out on one of the greatest, most timeless film mockumentaries ever made. The guitar amps of *Spinal Tap* go to 11, because any fool knows that's one louder than going to 10. In numerology, 11 is a master number that symbolizes inspiration, illumination, and spiritual enlightenment. One of my mottos is *You are what you believe.* If you believe something as simple as the number 11 can boost your positivity, then it will. Fans of the number 11 get a thrill up and down our spines when we notice 11:11 on our clocks. You can Google down a deep rabbit hole to debate the spiritual and numerological significance this number holds for seekers on the path to greater knowledge and purpose in their lives. For me, the people I've met who love to contact each other directly at 11:11 (a.m. or p.m.) are sending a simple message that says, "I see you. I get you. And we're all in this life together." Consider this book my 11:11 message to you.

Each of the 11 strategies are designed to take you from any current state of confusion about what's next to a new destination that will become clear and achievable once you work through the limitations that have been holding you back. The pain of losing your job can often feel like a fatal blow that you didn't see coming. You may not have survived your last job, but there's a happier shock to your system if you allow yourself to believe you've just lost something that can be replaced by work that's far greater.

There's not enough time to think about the future when the pressures of any present moment are all consuming. But the minute you're out of work, you've got an abundance of free time that can both scare you and inspire you, depending on the choices you make—choices that are now completely in your control. Do I wallow? Do I squander? Or do I regroup, recharge, reimagine, reinvent, and win? This is not a book about wishing and hoping. This is a book about taking the smartest practical steps on the right road to what's next.

I've learned that the largest salary is never on top of everyone's wish list. Workplace happiness may sound like a naive pipe dream, but there is a common desire inside the hearts and minds of candidates that's greater than money. The job seekers I work with agree on these points:

1. No more assholes. They want to work for people they can respect and trust.

2. A job that lines up with what they really want, without settling.

Reasonable aspirations. But it takes two to tango, and this book gives you the tools to do your part, working toward what you really want. Know what to ask for, how to ask for it, where to look, and what to require before you say, "Yes."

We start the journey to your next job by working through the shock and pain of job loss. In chapter 2, we race to your emotional rescue with life-saving survival steps to make sure the hardship that stole your income does not steal your sanity, your health, your relationships, and your life. In chapter 3, we tackle communication breakdowns with bosses and coworkers. A toxic workplace can breed bad actors. We'll give you strategies for getting more support and taking more responsibility next time.

The search to find your North Star, and your best job is not a million miles away. It's in chapter 4. Our strategy walks you through three easy steps from your heart to your head and into the proof that you have the experience to earn the work you're meant to be doing. Once you've set your sights on your North Star, chapter 5 forges the confidence to overcome objections to selling yourself in the most effective way to every potential employer. In chapter 6, you learn how to reach beyond your own four walls and the four corners of your damn digital screens to find a tribe of like-minded pros to maximize your opportunities and make the essential connections leading to the next job. There's power in numbers.

Social media may sound like the worst place to be wasting time during a productive job search, but one of the most important strategies to getting hired puts social media to work in a new way for you in chapter 7. You'll refine your own voice to promote your new professional brand and start rocking the relevant social platforms to build visibility. In chapter 8, you'll find a long list of mistakes to avoid—and best methods to adopt during every step of your search. The strategy in chapter 9 sets you up to nail the perfect thirty-minute job interview. Then you're ready to "close like a pro" in chapter 10, utilizing the best negotiation tactics to seal a deal and start your new job.

Chapter 11 is all about getting rich in spirit. We can be heroes when we take one minute, one hour, or one day away from our own struggles and reach out to people starving for the knowledge of lessons you've learned. You can lift people out of the darkness and into a fighting chance to get their lives back on track by devoting part of your time to helping someone who is hurting more than you. I hope you'll share these strategies with people you love who need help now.

Every word of this book came from the mind and heart of a man who had been stuck without any clear answers to find the right work and provide for the people I love. That person still lives inside me as a reminder of who I used to be before I started working with fellow seekers to find the right path. Clarity, purpose, focus, and rewards all arrive as the end results of making a decision to set your course to your unique new North Star. The ability to make this decision is inside you, but it's likely hidden by the stress that led you to pick up this book. Let me help replace that stress with hope, excitement, and determination.

DON'T JUST READ IT; USE IT—SHARE IT.

CHAPTER 1

It's Not "Just Business"

If you've ever been on the receiving end of this soul-sucking cliché, then you know how the first words of this awful speech begin: "What I'm about to say is *not* personal . . . it's just business."

I've suffered through being fired with this lame line more times than I would have liked. When you walk in to a meeting with your boss and you're surprised to see the head of human resources there as well, you're not about to get good news. The initial quiet is deafening. You may get a fake opening preamble that masquerades as friendly small talk: "I can't believe that rain today. Did you have as much trouble commuting into work as I did?" Sure, let's all pretend the roof is not about to come crashing down.

And then comes the "It's not personal" routine. Any boss who drops this bomb is unable or unwilling to summon the empathy and compassion needed to fire a person in a dignified way. All of us who have been through this rite of passage know that it's not only personal, it's primal. Deep emotional buttons are pushed when somebody strips away your income. A rush of stress begins to rain down and time slows to a crawl as you struggle to absorb the shock.

The world's worst opening line is usually followed by a carefully scripted speech about why the judge and jury are about to sentence you to death by firing squad. You'll know in the first few words whether you're about to get version 1 or version 2 of what my friend Lee likes to call: "Bye bye in the car car." Version 1 is the "It's not you, it's us," speech. As firing squads go, these bullets still kill, but they're far less painful than those discharged in version 2. When the company takes the blame, you don't have to sit there and suffer through all the accusations of what you've done wrong that led to this fateful moment. In version 1 of the firing speech, the company made the decision to let you go due to their own problems.

The person delivering the firing speech intends for this meeting to end as quickly as possible. You won't hear a long-winded tale outlining all the factors that led the company to terminate your employment, but you will get at least one specific reason for this final farewell. A few of the most popular old war horses include:

> ➤ I wish we could have done something to avoid this decision, but the last quarter of business fell far short of what we projected, and it's going to be impossible to keep you on the payroll right now.

➤ Our new CEO decided to make significant changes to the organization and this involves a restructuring, which eliminates three management positions in our branch, including yours.

➤ I hate to be the one to tell you this, but we've just learned that our company has been acquired by a private equity firm that has decided to stop manufacturing our entire line of products. They are going to sell off all of our assets. We're all getting exit packages, and I need to walk you through the details.

Every example of the "version 1" speech adds up to the same unhappy ending, with some solace sprinkled on top: "You're *out*, but it's not your fault." Version 2 of the firing speech is infinitely worse. In version 2, the liability for the termination is placed on you. It *is* your fault. The charges will be read in a cold, dead voice making it absolutely clear that a final decision has already been made and nothing you can say will be able to reverse it.

Here are some examples:

➤ I'm sorry to let you know it's come to this, but we've received a number of complaints about your performance from your supervisor and two of your coworkers. They all feel that you're no longer producing the quality of work that we need to keep you here on the job. We talked to you about this in your last performance review and let you know that if we didn't see more improvement we were going to have to make a change.

➤ I received a very disappointing phone call late last night. Your supervisor called to tell me that we've just lost a brand-new client due to complete mismanagement of the job you were hired to take on only eight weeks ago. I'm told that you refused to give us any warning that these people were flying off the rails. We just lost a $1.2 million deal. I have no choice but to tell you that your employment is being terminated immediately.

If you're in a situation where you think the ax is about to fall, the best thing you can do is summon every ounce of calm, breathe deeply, and do not lose your shit. Resistance is futile. The most important next step after the bomb drops is to maintain the greatest odds of getting the most favorable exit conditions.

In version 2, where you've been fired for cause, there's very little you can do except quickly suck it up and try not to further inflame the exit by freaking out. You've lost all leverage to negotiate for much (if anything) while they're showing you to the door.

But in Job Loss version 1, your tone of voice is just as important as the carefully chosen words you use to respond. While it's true that you've lost the job, it's possible to gain more assistance and support on the terms of your exit. Surprise the hell out of the person delivering this death sentence by being the about-to-be-fired employee they never saw coming. In the most relaxed and professional voice you can muster (remember, this is for *you*, not for them), try to prioritize a perfect list of requests. Health care is your number one issue. If your employer was providing health coverage, find out how long they can extend it before your opportunity to purchase COBRA coverage begins. Severance is next. Do everything possible, on your own or with the help of a lawyer, to get the maximum amount of severance before you agree to sign any document to release the employer from liability.

Investigate unemployment the minute you hit the pavement to get the maximum amount of cash benefits as quickly as possible. And then budget how long your incoming potential cash can last before tapping into any savings. Even during the best economic times, face your finances head on and do your best to control your expenses within the first week or two of losing your job.

Your First Rodeo

If this is the first time you've ever lost a job, it can feel like an untamed, wild bucking bronco tossed you into the dirt. This nasty beast is dangerous enough to start charging right back at you and close in for the kill. But we're not going to let that happen. This book is filled with expert advice from steady hands and brave hearts who walked out of every rodeo alive. Survival after every firing helps grow tougher skin and a stronger backbone to get back on that horse and ride again.

When you're fired without warning, the shock can take weeks to wear off. Even if you saw the ax coming, losing your job brings you face-to-face with intense stress and pain. Getting fired for the first time can feel like a bullet shot into the core of your identity. But a surprise firing is almost better than the alternative. When you're in a company that's been sending up bad smoke signals about the possibility of firings, furloughs, and layoffs, you know you're working in a house on fire. Waiting to find out if you're one of the people about to get burned—for weeks, or months—is a slow torture none of us deserves.

Losing your job is a financial blow that also shakes your confidence and your self-identity. For many of us, just the simple idea of having to change jobs rocks our world. Maybe it's an age thing. Most of the twentysomethings I work with aren't obsessed with staying at one company until retirement. They've grown up in the gig economy without the expectation of working in the same job for a long period of time before exploring what else is out there. Here's an imagined letter that twentysomething me could have written in the present day:

Dear Mom & Dad,

I've been meaning to write to you since the moment I lost my job. I've been hiding out, not reaching out to anyone. Thank you for all the times you tried to teach me about having a good work ethic, about trying to do my best, about how to act professionally, and about how to keep my cool when things get a little too hot.

You have no idea how crazy it got. Working for these people has been hell. Every single day felt like torture. The managers had no respect for the fact that everyone on our team was working twelve-hour days, nonstop for the last year. Not one of us got a raise or even a thank-you. We got constant demands to keep delivering, mixed with ongoing warnings about losing our jobs if we didn't perform up to their unrealistic expectations.

The minute I finally got scheduled for what I thought was going to be a performance review and a raise, they dropped the bomb on me saying that I was being let go.

Why is the work world so insane? How did the two of you keep the same jobs for as long as you did? Don't worry about me. I'll be fine once I figure out how to shake this off. They gave me four weeks of severance, which was about two weeks more than I expected. But at the risk of sending you both into shock, I have enough money saved up to pay rent without starving.

Talk soon.

Love,
Rob

Some of us define who we are by the job we hold. Our sense of purpose, responsibility, accountability, and drive to provide for our basic needs are all tied up in the work we do. It's also an easy way for others to define us. Most casual small talk only takes a minute before you're asked: "What do you do for a living?" If this is the first time you have had to dodge this attempt at sizing you up, welcome to a club that millions of us join.

Déjà Vu

If you've been kicked out of a job before, every bad memory of the hardships you suffered during your last time stuck in between jobs, again (#iBJA) can come racing back to haunt you. If bad fortune comes back multiple times in your career, getting kicked out of work *again* can trigger the original earthquake, with every aftershock that followed. It's normal to feel overwhelmed if this is happening to you now. But we have new strategies to get you through this. The ground will stop shaking. The roof will not collapse.

Don't let sad scenes from your last time out of work start playing over and over in your head. Erase this rerun and start writing a brand-new script called *The First Time I Lost My Job Without Losing My Mind*. It's too long a title, but it's going to be a much better sequel. Job loss can unravel everything you have, think, and feel, *or* losing your job can ignite a reevaluation of purpose and value. This is a chance to find the work you're meant to do.

This is your moment to overcome the temporary hell of being fired, furloughed and sent home by using a new strategic plan to get hired in the shortest amount of time. The old ways of looking for work don't cut it anymore. After some of the worst economic times in history, you can feel stuck in a sea of unemployed souls treading water without a life preserver. The worn-out methods people have utilized for decades won't cure today's conditions. New road-tested tools help you rethink how to best position yourself, and write a better blueprint to win your next, best job.

Your Evil Twin

I know what you're going through. Being out of work always made me feel like I was tied down in chains. The walls felt like they were closing in. I was sentenced to serve time in solitary confinement without any idea how long it was going to take to get out of unemployment prison. The weight of all that stress ate away at my strength and confidence.

As smart as I thought I was, I felt like I was back in grade school, staring at a math problem that was impossible to solve. I felt even worse about the idea that I was letting my family down, ashamed that my loss was placing a heavy burden on the people I love. They weren't used to seeing me around all the time, every damn day and night. And they definitely weren't used to seeing me constantly worried about every dollar we thought about spending.

If you normally have an all-caps EGO, that sucker shrinks down to lower case letters the minute you lose your job. If you're singing the "It Sucks to Be Me" blues, you're not the first one to belt out this tune. There are endless other travelers out of work right now, all on the same lonesome highway, hoping to catch a ride to the promised land where a shiny new job and a pretty paycheck awaits.

Being fired can feel like losing half of who you are. Or, you might sense that you've gained an evil twin; a sadder, quieter, angry, confused, and frustrated you can show up like an unwanted guest. If this twin refuses to take every hint to leave, you're in for more serious trouble. Sad-Quiet-Angry-You will start inviting more imaginary friends over to this pity party. Here comes Fear, Anxiety, and a terrifying final guest named Panic. We're going to help you kick every one of these horrible houseguests the hell out before any of them find a hiding place and stick around for good.

Counting Friends

One of the hardest lessons learned when you fall in between jobs is finding out the difference between real friends ready to help and people who don't show up when you need them most. This moment demands real friends. I'm sorry if you were counting on more former coworkers and colleagues to reach out. The first few times I was let go, this disappointment became an unhealthy obsession. *How could Steve not call? We spent hours working together every day for the past two years and I still haven't gotten one text? Maybe he's been in a car accident? Maybe he's overwhelmed with survivor's guilt? Maybe the past two years of our friendship were a lie?*

Real friends never treat you like a disease they don't want to catch. True friends don't worry they may not have the perfect words to say. They show up to listen and let you know your bond is beyond what you can do for each other professionally. The people who care about you when it counts are unconditional teammates for life. It's okay if you can only count these superheroes on one hand. You need real friendship now like oxygen.

One of the internal debates that comes up when you lose a job is wondering whether the relationships you formed with people at work were transactional, or whether there was something deeper, a friendship that transcends all the scratching and the clawing that happens in the workplace. I don't think transactional relationships are dirty or bad. They can be clear and effective, if you're honest with each other. It's okay to ask someone for what you need. It's less okay to need help and simply assume the other person is going to read your mind. It's even crazier to get upset if they don't.

We've got to learn to ask. If the motivations and intentions behind the ask are true and clear, then the worst that can happen is a pass. And when someone you need steps up and chooses to help in a meaningful way, please respect, remember, and look for every opportunity to return that support when your friend needs you down the line.

The Doctor Will See You Now

If you're hurt badly in a car accident, you get to a doctor immediately. If you're knocked unconscious playing sports, you're carried off on a stretcher. Job doctors, headhunters, recruiters, and career coaches can be the best resources to help you let the healing begin. I know a great one (who looks a lot like me). Reach out. The right job doc can help you get your head screwed back on straight. The investment you're willing to make in these professional services can come back many times over if you get sage advice and the best résumé and selling materials you need. Professional job docs can get you the right contacts and placement services much faster than you could have done without their input and expertise.

If you're feeling too down to make these moves, you might be well served to share the news of losing your job with your primary care physician. This kind of stress can immediately impact your body and your mind. The constant pressure to get a new job as quickly as possible can send the mind racing at unhealthy speeds, and good decisions are rarely made in a panicked state. If you're not careful, the weight of these burdens—and the fear produced by not knowing where your next paycheck is coming from—can create unhealthy new habits as well as depression, anxiety and sleep disruption. Your doctor can prescribe medication if you decide it's needed to help unburden your state of mind and ease your suffering.

If you have any tendency to overuse and abuse alcohol and drugs, please consider getting the help you need now. If you're having outbursts of anger and rage, your heart and soul need healing you may not be able to get without reaching out to a professional. This help can prevent you from hurting the people you love, the people you need now as much as they need you.

If the grief, self-defeat, and hopelessness ever feel like too much to handle on your own, please consider professional therapy. The right therapist will help stop your life from spinning out of control. Ask everyone who loves you to help do the research and make recommendations. I went through a personal tragedy and the loss of a job at the same time. Crisis counseling introduced me to the therapist who helped me put my life back together. I was surprised and elated to learn that my therapist had a policy shared by many others: to offer drastically reduced fees to a number of patients in dire need—and for some patients, no fee at all. *Ask.*

The F Words

F words like *fired* or *furloughed* can easily turn into *fear.*

Fear has the power to wound deeply and leave scars that can flare up anytime your survival instincts are triggered by a threat. Fear attacks confidence. And fear can form a suit of armor that surrounds your heart, convincing you the only way to avoid more pain is to hide from another battle. Please don't be afraid of your new job search. This fear can kill your career.

I used to check my bank account balances a dozen times a day after getting fired. I would gaze at the

25

It's about grabbing hold of your
anger and moving beyond
"Why me?" to attack the more
essential question, "What's next?"

dollars on my phone app like an ancient wizard trying to summon the mystic power to command the numbers not to shrink. Then I'd shift focus to what was in the refrigerator. I would rather think about what snack to eat next (to feed the fear) than go back to solving the problems at hand. A nap always sounded good. Sure, I'd feel a little guilty, but a guy needs to be well-rested to get things done, right? All of these delay tactics enabled me to run away from the reality of being out of work.

The fight-or-flight response is full proof that you're human. While a flight might appear to be more comfortable, your future is worth the fight. At the outset of losing a job, the enemies are all external. The minute you're home alone, the new challenge is to learn how to identify all the internal enemies and fight back for what you need and what you deserve. I'm going to give you the tools to do just that.

All the financial stress, social isolation, deflection, and distraction can boil into an explosion of anger. I had the thrill of learning a lot about anger when I worked with John Lydon, aka Johnny Rotten. We co-created a show for VH1 in the '90s called *Rotten TV*. One of John's must-read autobiographies (the one with me in it) is called *Anger Is an Energy*. We can use the angry energy of getting fired for a righteous purpose—to learn how to regain our superpowers in the time it takes to read this book. It's time to become the Boss of Badass Job Searching and overcome the agony of defeat. It's about transmutation. It's about getting up off the mat. It's about grabbing hold of your anger and moving beyond "Why me?" to attack the more essential question, "What's next?"

Change is the better alternative to being pissed. It's always personal and never "just business." If there is only one thing you take away from my book, it's this: You've got a curable disease that does not have to last for months and months. You have the decision-making power to chart the right course and the ability to take control of your own job search like a super-ninja.

CHAPTER 2

Emotional Rescue

When I was living in Dallas in my twenties, I met one of the wisest souls I've ever known, who taught me two lessons I've carried through every hard time since. I was invited, along with about a dozen other seekers, to a weekly question-and-answer session held in a private home downtown. We sat around this brilliant man—pastor, theologian, musician, and devoted educator, Father A. A. Taliaferro. Every Tuesday night, we would ask him questions about the purpose and meaning of existence. We were lucky to be listening to someone who'd spent his whole life studying the keys to the universe—and he was using those keys to unlock answers to questions we were dying to ask.

One evening, he introduced us to a secret group in the hope that we might join. He called it the Worrier's Club. Anyone who sought entry would be granted access as long as they agreed to just one condition: We would be allowed to worry our heads off, but only for five minutes each day, because worrying accomplishes absolutely nothing.

On another night, the second greatest lesson learned came in only two words. I was suffering emotional pain over a series of recent losses, and I asked Father Taliaferro a question. I looked at him with what remained of my earnest hope: "Why is there so much pain?" He gazed back at me for a long time. I felt like he looked right through me . . . and he said, "To learn."

You can't think clearly about what's next when you're in too much pain after losing a job. Coming up with the right solution takes time and positive energy you may not have. Clarity can only arrive after healing. Once you find a way out, ideas and inspiration start to flow again, and you can work with a renewed sense of purpose about the next steps to take.

Father Taliaferro helped me realize that pain was a perfect teacher waiting for me to listen and learn how to turn hardship into new possibilities. I had thought suffering was the enemy, but Father Taliaferro helped me realize that my angst was the professor holding answers to what came next. Thirty years later, I met another teacher who reminded me of the same lesson. When I worked with Joe Biden, he showed me how to turn pain into purpose.

We've all heard stories about people who suffer serious addictions and decide to quit cold turkey, without any help or a process to reduce their addiction gradually. If you've got the supreme strength to wish the pain of job loss away in an instant, you're among the lucky few. Like many of us, I wasn't able to get over the withdrawal symptoms of losing jobs cold turkey. I needed a process to help me heal.

Here are the survival tools I used to soothe the suffering—tools that can help you from falling into common traps and lose months of valuable time. These steps can help you avoid the dangerous downward spiral of a job loss and restore sanity, balance, strength and focus.

My Top 11 Self-Care Rituals

Here's my Top 11 list of self-care rituals to help you stay sane:

Survival Step 1:
Meditate

If meditation has been a part of your life before, this is the best moment to bring it back—for at least twenty minutes every day. Sitting peacefully, without any agenda except the repetition of calm breathing, is one of the simplest pleasures of being alive. Don't critique your ability to block every negative thought from invading your lovely head. You miss out on the maximum benefits of meditation by letting an ounce of judgment in. When random thoughts invade your no-thought zone, let them make a brief cameo, and then let them fly off the very second after they appear. Take another breath and let the random thinking go. Don't believe you're not doing it right. You're doing it right. Breathe. Sit. Relax.

Richard Alpert was a prominent Harvard psychologist. He found his true calling as Ram Dass, a spiritual teacher and humanitarian who gave millions of soul seekers a loving key to understanding existence and knowing peace, with three words to solve all that ails you:

BE HERE NOW.

Not then, not when, not if, not why, not how . . .

Just HERE, just NOW, just BE.

Your body needs rest and sleep. Your mind and spirit need love and caring. By practicing meditation, you gift yourself a daily ritual for quieting the mind and refreshing the spirit. Meditation opens doors of intuition that may be closed.

Some people prefer to follow a specific method. You can create your own. There is no wrong way to allow your mind and spirit to rest and relax if you just let go of thoughts, tasks, worries, responsibilities, hopes, dreams, or fears. Twenty or more minutes each day will give you back the peace of mind you're missing now and renew your strength.

For many people, it's helpful to pick a favorite, regular spot to meditate. Wherever you decide to sit, make sure you're in a position that's comfortable. Close your eyes and focus on slow and easy long breaths. Your mental stress needs an escape valve and meditation is a simple way to release all the pressure. There are many apps available to try: *Waking Up* by Sam Harris, *Ten Percent*

Happier by ABC's Dan Harris (no relation), *Headspace*, *Breethe* (correct spelling), *Calm*, and *Insight Timer*.

Survival Step 2:
Fire the "No" Police

No. You're not going to be able to find a good job for a long time.

No. You can't find a better job with higher pay.

No. You're too junior.

No. You're too senior.

No. You have to settle for less.

No. This is the worst time to find a new job.

No. You're not qualified.

These self-defeating bad cops will stay in your head as long as you let the anger and sadness of recent job loss mix with fear. The "No" Police enter without a warrant and you have the right to ask them to leave. The first bad cop fills your head with: *It's going to take forever to find your next job. It's going to be hard, embarrassing, and you may not succeed.* Take every cliché and negative prediction you've ever heard about how long it will take for you to find a job and please, flush them away. The minute you start telling yourself that it's going to take at least five months to find the right job is the minute you start conditioning your mind to think it can't go any faster. No matter how high the unemployment numbers might be at any moment, you are always one human being away from getting the right opportunity.

Don't make deadly declarations about your job prospects based on where you live. "There aren't enough jobs in Cleveland right now." Blanket statements like this are useless. You need much more nutritious brain fuel than that to build back the confidence it's going to take to be able to present yourself to the right people at the right companies.

Survival Step 3:
Exorcise the Demons

Like the "No" Police, demons of all kinds can sneak into your head on a daily basis. They can be tenacious and pervasive. It's like Whac-A-Mole, and you need to be armed with multiple strategies for keeping the tidal wave of potential negativity at bay. When your guard is down, you're susceptible to attack from all the dark parts of your own mind. It's natural to summon up these fears and worries. But if you start to grant them too much time and real estate, you're asking for even more trouble by letting this primal noise take on more power than it deserves. The devil inside can spread evil thoughts and insults like these tragically familiar psychic tropes:

You should be ashamed of yourself for losing that job.

You're never going to get another job in this economy.

You know you're going to get passed over for every
job by someone much younger.

You'll never have enough new skills to be hired by
anyone.

You're going to have to take a radical pay cut just to
find a job.

Those are just a few examples of the more vicious, internal assaults that can rise up when you're down. Create a daily ritual to exorcise these devilish attacks on your confidence. Consider doing some important mental gymnastics first thing in the morning every day you're out of work. Write down a few of the horrible lies your devil says about what a loser you've become and then burn those lies up in smoke. No, really. Go outside every morning with a lighter, a piece of paper, and a pen or pencil. Write down any of the worst attacks that might come out of your devil brain, whatever they might be:

You're too old.

Nobody gives a damn about you.

You're never going to be able to pay the rent.

You can't afford your daughter's college tuition and
you're about to ruin her life.

You're going to have to file for bankruptcy.

Those five fears will do for now. There'll be plenty more conjured up every day. Write down every evil idea and read all your lies out loud. You can adopt a nasty, devilish tone of voice if you want to really lay on the disgust and get into this ritual. Crumple up that piece of paper with gusto. Lay it on the ground. Light it up. And watch it burn.

You may feel like an idiot, but a physical ritual like this is an active way to make sure you're telling yourself not to give in to your fears. Don't let fears turn into realities. Burn 'em. Humans have practiced rituals forever. This simple routine can neutralize and exorcise your demons.

Survival Step 4:
Cure Ageism

The minute you stop believing that everyone will see you as too old for the job, you won't be. Ageism is a prison in your own mind. Break out of this jail immediately. If you're telling yourself and everyone who'll listen that you're not going to find a job because you're too old, you've already given up on the idea that you can outshine the competition.

You can cure ageism when you're more positive, effective, motivating, likable, attractive, smart, fun, inspiring, generous, confident, strong and approachable than candidates of any age. Fill the room with super-charged, magnetic energy and it's difficult for people to focus on rejecting you regardless of your age.

I can make a list of hundreds of people who don't think of themselves as "old." They don't act old, they don't feel old, they are *not* old. Pete Townsend wrote about hoping to die before he got old when he was twenty. But Pete is still scoring rock anthems and smashing guitars at the ripe, young age of seventy-five (as of this writing). Two words: Betty White. If age is the problem, then intuition, inspiration and intensely brilliant ideas are the antidotes. Drop the idea that you're "too old" by being too excellent to lose.

Too old? No.

Too unfocused? Maybe.

Not enough singing from the rooftops? Yeah.

Too much worry? For sure.

Not enough confidence? Most definitely.

But these things can be fixed.

People filled with fire and passion, ideas, and constant forward motion to solve any issue in the workplace are ageless. Let that person be you. Be the strongest candidate for the job whether your fear brain is telling you that you're too old, too young, too thin, too fat. Cut the crap and *be you*.

Don't get me wrong: Ageism does exist. There's plenty of evidence to support the fact that many companies secretly decide to hire the candidates who are younger and more affordable over people who bring a greater level of experience along with the need for a higher salary. But ageism is a disease of the mind. The more you start listening to this fear, the more power you give it by worrying about it, the more your confidence weakens.

What's in your heart and in your mind is ageless.

It comes down to one simple idea: The people you're supposed to be working with get you, need you, and want you in the job. Those who don't are not the people you should be working with anyway.

Survival Step 5:
Commit to Date Night

One of the best survival steps is to challenge yourself to not let more than seven days pass without going out on at least one great date. Going on a date is about getting out, having an adventure, and getting your mind off the job search. When you spend most of your unemployed minutes stuck inside, the isolation can be overwhelming. You may not feel like you've got the right stuff to turn the socializing part of your brain on right now, but having some fun is vital. Make a plan, at least once a week, to get out with someone who believes in fun. Any money you spend on a date is a worthy investment to sustain sanity. You can date as creatively and inexpensively as you like, as long as you make the decision to not let the dating muscles fade away. If you don't have a willing partner, or anyone you want to see, take yourself out for a solo date and make fun happen like your life depended on it.

The age of COVID-19 pushed us all to create new ways to break away from too much isolation. Walks and hikes became viable, desirable ways to socialize. When I lived in New York City, I used to hit the streets and walk for miles without any planned destination. The constant influx of city energy was always enough to stop my mind from spinning that endless loop of troubles tied to being out of work.

Making the commitment to maintain your dating life can do more than just keep you sane. The stress of being out of work can put serious strain on your relationships and your marriage. Be careful not to get stuck too far inside yourself that you're forgetting to make time for the people you love. And if you're not getting the love you want and need, be careful not to let that pain turn into anger; ask your partner for the time and attention to feed your hungry heart.

Survival Step 6:
Endorphin-ize

During the first weeks after losing your job, you may just want to curl up inside a blanket. Crushing statistics show that opioid use skyrockets when unemployment rises. It's too easy to think you need to ease the pain with just one more drink, or one more dose of something you know you should be keeping in check. Take the safer roads provided by nature. Healthy meds ignite the much-needed regular rush of chemicals to get your mojo working. These fixes are easier, cheaper, and more effective than any pill. Here's a starter list to soothe your soul and let the endorphins flow:

- Passionate Sex

- Vigorous Exercise

- Dark Chocolate

- Spontaneous Dance

- Music Marathons

- Blissful Massage

- Steam or Sauna Sweat Fests

Practicing any of these endorphin-boosting methods will radically erase the false belief that you are incapable of enjoying life simply because you're unemployed. The people responsible for taking away your last job do not get to steal your soul. *Those people* are "just business," this stuff "is personal."

Survival Step 7:
Recruit a Super Sponsor

One of the best ways to make sure you're using any of these survival steps without slipping or falling into despair is to deputize at least one trusted friend to be your Super Sponsor. Pick someone who knows you best and ask them to promise to make regularly scheduled check-ins to keep you accountable for making legitimate positive progress every day. Face-to-face visits from a friend you can count on are ideal, but phone calls, video chats, emails, or texts will all give you the consistent, supportive nudge you need to stay on track.

People who care about you will often say something like, "Please let me know if there's anything I can do to help." Being a Super Sponsor is a perfect answer. It's a lot easier than asking friends for a loan. And if you make this request as simple and specific as possible, you'll increase the odds that the person you ask will easily say yes.

Imagine something as basic as a once-a-week check-in—for five to fifteen minutes—to talk about what progress you've made on the job search, and to give you feedback and ideas about how to keep forward momentum going. Adding this friend to your job search SWAT team gives you the regular accountability you need to solve the situation.

Tackling this entire process on your own can create a negative echo chamber. Bringing a trusted friend into the mix, at least once every week while you're out of work, gives you the ability to bounce all of your ideas off someone who's invested in making sure you're taking meaningful steps forward. Your Super Sponsor will catch you when you're falling and lift you up to make constructive, constant progress.

Survival Step 8:
Volunteer

When you're out of work and worried about having no income, an unwanted sales call, even from a charitable organization, can elicit dread and a touch of guilt if you feel like you're in no place to contribute cash to help someone else.

When I was eliminated from my last job, I got a call from a friend asking if I was interested in joining a group of advisers in a charity organization I'd known about since childhood. WhyHunger (WhyHunger.org) was founded by Bill Ayres and Harry Chapin in the 1970s to end world hunger. The opportunity to get to work immediately for a greater good gave me a positive way to fill the overabundance of empty hours on my hands. I started donating my time working with a team of people who needed as much of my talent as I could give. I got a chance to recapture some of the creative energy that I was missing. I made new contacts and found a selfless way to re-engage with all my previous connections for the higher purpose of supporting a just cause.

It's not hard to look around for people in need—in your community, in your city, state, country, or beyond all borders—to find those in much more difficult and dire circumstances than you. Any amount of time and energy you can devote to helping people who need your support will take you out of your head and straight into the hearts of others. Your contribution of time and effort yields the priceless energy and sense of purpose that may be missing in your own life right now.

Once you feel this kind of positive energy, your entire outlook can shift. Your smile returns. Your pace quickens. Your own worries disappear when you're too busy helping someone who needs you. Your good works transform into a more magnetic version of yourself—and you'll start attracting more positive thoughts and new people.

Survival Step 9:
Practice the Murray Rule

Murray was the father of one of my best friends. He was a classic, old school, traveling salesman. Murray used to preach that when you're at your lowest, when your stress levels are off the charts, when there's absolutely no way you can justify spending any money on fun and entertainment . . . you're at the exact right moment to unleash "The Murray Rule." Scrape together the fewest dollars possible and spend your way into some momentary maximum fun. Go to a movie. Get ice cream. Buy something cheap and stupid online. Revel in spending just a few dollars to kill the lie in your head making you think you'll never make another dollar again.

The Murray Rule is a paranoia destroyer. And if you're still too frugal to take down your fear flag with some righteous shopping therapy, you can still create a weekly escape from your job search by spending mental capital on figuring out how to make instafun happen in a cashless way to heal the hardships. Murray is looking down from the great beyond, begging you to rob your own cookie jar.

Survival Step 10:
Calendarize

The least sexy app on your phone deserves much more respect than it gets. Your calendar is your most important tool to lessen the time you're going to be out of work, and prioritize the right steps to win your next, best job.

When your daily schedule largely belonged to the company you worked for, your calendar was filled with meetings, zooms, and calls from coworkers and employers asking you to spend tons of time talking and talking and talking about the work you were all supposed to be doing, instead of doing the actual work. (That's one thing you probably don't miss about being employed.) Once you fall in between jobs, your calendar is rather naked. Your schedule starts to look like one of those dusty, one-horse ghost towns in an old western movie. Tumbleweeds blow by, the wind whistles, skies turn gray, and there isn't a single meeting with another cowgirl or cowboy anywhere in sight.

If you're trying to create anything new in your life, something meaningful that seems elusive, ask yourself what actions you're taking every single day to make that happen. If you don't commit to scheduling time to work on all the individual essential elements of a successful job search every day, your search is going to drag on without an ending you can predict.

Your calendar is your most important tool to lessen the time you're going to be out of work, and prioritize the right steps to win your next, best job.

When I'm in between jobs, my calendar is sacred ground. I imagine I've got the most demanding boss I've ever worked for—*me*. If I schedule a "meeting" on my calendar, it's mandatory. No last-minute cancellations. No endless postponements and rescheduling. When the boss schedules a meeting, you've got to be there on time, every time. This level of discipline is going to transform your job search into a much more productive daily ritual. Decide what time you want to start your workday every morning and make sure there's a meeting on your schedule at that same time on all weekdays. At the beginning of your search, most of these meetings take place with your favorite person on earth—you. As you reach out to more prospects every day, interviews with potential hiring managers will start filling up your calendar.

Here's a sample of what a day at the onset of your job search journey can look like. These scheduled events are examples of how to get busy, focused, and productive without a single job interview set . . . yet.

Your pace and style may not match this particular example. The point is to build your own version of a full schedule with productive, repeatable activities that will quickly become your new routine. If you adopt some of the ideas that resonate the best, you'll replace more solo time by meeting directly with hot prospects:

TODAY

9:00 a.m.   Meditate.

9:20 a.m.   Calendarize A's & B's (ten minutes that will change your life, see below).

9:30 a.m.   Read up on any breaking news in your industry.

10:00 a.m. Post your first professional social media of the day and reply, like, and share other posts with the most engaging content relating to your line of work. (There are plenty of scheduling apps if you'd prefer to plan these in advance. See chapter 7, "Social Voodoo.")

10:20 a.m. Get the hell off social media.

10:25 a.m. I'm not kidding. Turn your social apps off.

10:26 a.m. Review and update your list of target companies you're researching (see chapter 8).

11:00 a.m. Fifteen-minute bio break: water, snacks, smiling, fresh air.

11:15 a.m. Review current and most recent job listings at your target companies.

Noon   Email top prospects (only if you have direct connections). Email others in your network to get the direct connections you still need.

1:00 p.m.   Lunch.

1:30 p.m.   Email catch-up. Are you in shock that I waited until 1:30 p.m.? Here's why: Obsessively checking email every minute of the day is the single greatest productivity killer. By scheduling a few email sessions with yourself (2–3 per day), you'll massively reduce the desperation energy and significantly increase time spent making strategic moves to win the fight. Be less reactive. Be more focused.

1:50 p.m.   Post your second professional social media of the day and reply, like, and share other posts that have already caught a lot of attention.

2:10 p.m.   Get off all your apps. No . . . really.

2:11 p.m.   Not kidding.

2:12 p.m.   Homework: Take approximately forty-five minutes here to do any and all research on one of the target companies on your list that has a current job opening you want.

3:00 p.m.   Fifteen-minute bio break: water, snacks, smiling, fresh air.

3:15 p.m.   Email catch-up.

3:30 p.m.   Review A's & B's (see below).

3:40 p.m.   Email more top prospects if you have direct connections. Email others in your network to get the direct connections you still need.

4:15 p.m.   Review and update your list of target companies based on emails sent/received.

4:30 p.m.   Friend Zone: Get a blast of good energy going by reaching out to people you love. No whining.

4:50 p.m.   Post your third professional social media of the day and reply, like, and share other posts that have already caught a lot of attention.

5:00 p.m.   Final email catch-up.

5:25 p.m.   Review & update target company spreadsheet. Review & Reset A's & B's for tomorrow.

If you're looking at the example above and thinking there's no way that you would ever want to schedule every minute of your day out of work, you'll get no judgment from me. But making a schedule is one of the most surefire ways of making forward progress. I promise I won't sound like a diet coach throughout the book, but I'm about to sound a little bit like a diet coach now. If you're like me, then you're looking down at your gut wishing you could lose a few pounds. I'll paraphrase Sting to say that every move I make to eat less and exercise more is going to move me in the right direction. The same thing goes for your job search. Scheduling your day and committing to a system will help you start taking the steps forward so you can walk right into your next best job.

Use any of these ideas above to begin blocking out the working hours of your job search. Toss any concepts that don't feel right. But adapt a real plan to prime you to excel in your new role: President of Getting a Job, Inc.

Stick to a firm schedule and you'll be miles ahead of job seekers floundering from hour to hour, waiting for miracles to land in their inbox. You'll also stave off a massive amount of dread and confusion by turning what normally feels like a painful daily slog into a focused mission each day.

Once you've done enough initial outreach (over several weeks) to start getting real responses, you will constantly alter the daily calendar to make room for meetings with the hottest prospects and the people with one degree of separation from the decision makers you have to reach.

Once you're past the first few weeks, I strongly advise you to level up your calendarization by putting the best time management system to work. My favorite method matches a lifelong lesson that the simplest concepts can also be the most profound, and this system is the easiest thing in the world to remember and practice. And all you'll need is a pen and a scratch pad.

ABC Time Management is not an app, it's a concept—a simple one, with the power to organize your job search. ABC prioritizes all of your daily work projects into three categories that are impossible to forget: A, B, or C. Once you learn how to use this idea, your calendar will help keep your eyes focused on the prize. You'll soon start prioritizing the tasks that bring the best odds for success.

Once you power through as many cups of morning coffee as you need, the first "meeting" on your schedule every day should not take more than ten minutes, if that. In this meeting, you're going to think strategically about all the tasks in front of you and break them down into three categories with the radical names: A B C.

Make an A list of no more than three of the most important work priorities you want to accomplish *today* to find your next, best job. Your A list is how you will spend the most valuable time of the day. An "A" priority beats out anything else on your potential list of projects.

Your B list is the next set of priorities you want to accomplish on this day's search. But you can't start working on a "B" until you've completed your A list on any one particular day.

The best rule about this ABC Time Management System is to never work on a C-level project. Think about your C list as the sad kid sitting on the bench wishing for a chance to be called into the game by the coach. If this was a child's game and I was the coach, I'd give every C kid a chance to play every day of the week. But you're not a kid anymore. You've just been kicked off the field and sent home from the big leagues. And now you need every one of your A and B players back on the field to win the next, best job. There's no time for a C project to sneak onto your daily calendar and take you away from working on A's and B's.

If your brain still flirts with working on a C, if something on your project list won't stop begging for attention, it's possible that pushy C is ready to become a B and make it onto today's schedule. *But I Doubt It.*

This time management system only works when you're able to prioritize an agenda to spend most of your job search hours working on the items with the best chance of leading you to meaningful interviews for actual open jobs.

Survival Step 11:
Remember the Taste
of the Magic Corn Muffin

I once lived in a tiny, one-room apartment in the mid-Wilshire section of Los Angeles. I was trying to figure out what was next after losing a job. There was a huge picture window in this studio looking right out at the Hollywood sign in the distance. This was ironic on so many levels. I'd come to Hollywood as one of a bazillion dreamers with an idea for a television show. But I realized that an ex–radio guy trying to get into television might need to find a way in at a lower level, forgetting about my success in the past, and climbing my way up again.

At my lowest point, on a dark day on the journey, I was about to give up all hope and get a job waiting tables. Then, like a scene in a movie, the phone rang. An old friend called to ask what I was doing. I said something lame like, "Conquering LA." I'd worked with my friend years before in rock radio. We kept in touch on and off over time. And now she was in a big job at one of the coolest places on the planet, MTV. She wanted to know if I was interested in coming to interview for a job on her team back in New York. That same day, I was actually getting ready to fly east for my best friend's wedding. I saved her from having to buy me a plane ticket. Fate, history, luck, timing, need, desire, and one person stepped in to change my life.

That phone call eventually led to almost twelve years working at MTV and VH1. I trekked three thousand miles back across the country to NYC and moved into another small apartment. I was subletting from a generous friend in Greenwich Village at 24 Fifth Avenue. This classic building stood tall, just two blocks in front of the classic arch at the gateway to Washington Square Park. It was magical. I'd get in the elevator early every morning, and when the elevator doors opened, there was a small newspaper stand inside the lobby. An extra-friendly, old New York guy was there selling coffee, newspapers . . . and corn muffins. God they were good.

My new job at MTV was uptown in a building at 57th and Broadway. It was summertime. Every morning, I'd get my coffee. I'd tuck a newspaper under my arm. I'd get my corn muffin. And I would walk from 9th to 57th Street. I'd been living away from the city for a dozen years at this point in my life. The return made me feel like a tourist, biting the Big Apple for the first time.

Over thirty years later, whenever life gets hard, I remember that new job spirit, walking to a gig that I loved, feeling confident and worshipping the perfect taste of a big, buttery corn muffin. It's a spirit you want to feel and recapture on any journey you're about to take from pain to purpose. You can't win again unless you remember what it feels like when you've won before. Feel it.

CHAPTER 3

Rise Up

Every survival step in chapter 2 can help you regain the confidence and optimism that was lost along with your last job. But before winning what's next, there's one more step to heal any anger, betrayal, and bitterness— all gifts of the recent past. Blaming people who may have done you wrong is completely expected. It can even feel like a warm blanket at times. But this mind-set is a major roadblock preventing you from rising up and getting hired faster. Anger and resentment are ties that bind you to the unemployment line if you don't untangle them. Your new job search is not a grudge match.

If bad-mouthing was an Olympic sport, I'm ashamed to say I'd have a lot of old medals hidden in my closet. It took me a while to realize that this behavior wasn't winning me any favors, and was actually preventing me from getting what I really wanted: winning great work to support my family. I want to share strategies that raise your emotional intelligence to handle conflicts that lead to meltdowns at work. If you realize why office politics devolved into situations that led to your job loss, you have power to purge that anger and lighten your load. Everyone brings some baggage into the workplace. Our upbringing and all our toughest work experiences get packed in suitcases we all lug around. I'm going to encourage you to dump these heavy bags filled with all the wrongs done to you in the past. If not, you're too susceptible to losing your cool during every stop on the job search journey. And you're going to have a dark cloud over your head throughout the race to get hired.

Everybody Hurts

Hierarchies exist in nature, and in work. No matter where you stand on the company ladder, you're always looking up at someone who's at least one rung above you. Even if you're the boss, you're going to experience times when you've gotta hum that Bob Dylan tune and "serve somebody."

If you had problems with anybody up or down the company ladder that brought about your recent downfall, this is the time to think through why those relationships blew up. Be as honest as you can about what you could have done differently.

Conflicts erupt in every company, and the reasons are rarely one-dimensional. Think about past meltdowns at work more like Spock and less like Kirk. Pile on a healthy dose of humility when analyzing your past working relationships. You're in the safe space of your own imagination, far from any HR watchdogs lurking around the corner to write up a nasty report.

The goal is not only to get over the anger of a job gone horribly wrong, but to learn how to reframe your stories during every job interview so that questions about the past don't bring stress and tension front and center. Show what you gained from previous work experience without attacking any backstabbers. It's the wrong move in any interview. (More on this in chapter 9.)

If you're as passionate a personality as I am, there's a dire need to summon up as much Vulcan as possible before starting your next job search. Your logical side paves the best path to the strategies that will get you hired quickly. Fiery emotions will trip you up and keep you in the volatile state of mind you felt when you lost your last job. This is the time to transcend your anger, forgive the past, and rewrite your future.

Meet the New Boss

Before you're ready to meet a new boss, you definitely want to make sure it's not going to be the same as the old boss if everything just ended up into crazy town on your last job. If you've been fired for cause, or let go by a boss who was unwilling to save your job, I want to arm you with more strategy to understand why this most important relationship at work can go off the rails. I want to give you more tools to improve your results dealing with management during interviews—and eventually in your next job.

This is the time to transcend your anger, forgive the past, and rewrite your future.

It's hard to find too many people willing to give past bosses glowing reviews. Bad bosses come in all shapes and sizes: the mood swinger, the puppet on a string, the phantom, the tyrant, the unfit. I'm planning to write an entire book about this special breed of professionals to help train a new class of better leaders. You're going to waste every ounce of rocket fuel burning empty calories if you keep raging about the person who fired you, without figuring out how to turn that energy into productive planning for what comes next.

If it's clear that your boss was the lone gunman who took you down, think hard about whether there was anything you could have done differently to prevent that from happening. If you suspect multiple people had fingers on the trigger, your primal need to want to fight back against them still won't change the outcome. You've been shitcanned. What happens next is all that matters. And the anger will hold you down unless you turn it into fresh wisdom.

At one point in my career, our chief executive was driving the management team crazy. None of us felt like we had more than an inch to initiate anything without 100 percent approval of every detail in advance. On the surface, this may not sound terrible, but when you're led by someone everyone pegs as a classic micromanager, the slow uncertain approval process of any project feels like you're holding a grenade with the pin pulled out.

Once, at the brink of total frustration, I confided in a trusted coworker to vent some of the angst of being second-guessed. At first, my teammate let me spew it all out. But once my points were made, he wanted me to understand something that my emotions and ego were allowing to get in the way.

Our boss had achieved tremendous success for decades. His micromanagement style driving me nuts was the same style he had been using for a long time before I entered the arena. That style worked fine for him. It just didn't work for me. I was working under the false assumption that I was going to cure our boss of a trait he had no interest in giving up. My friend said there were two choices: Leave or accept that this was the job I signed up for and figure out how to make it more workable.

A micromanager will be much less manic if you create a constant flow of information that keeps your boss in the know. A system of regular, proactive updates is the key to saving your sanity, and possibly your job.

Check Please

When I was fired during an earlier time in my career, it wasn't until years later that I was able to reflect on why it happened, and what I could've done differently to prevent an unhappy ending. A passive-aggressive relationship with my boss led to a disciplinary action I did not deserve. A minor issue was spun into a complaint designed to kick me to the pavement.

If you've ever felt like you faced the firing squad being unjustly accused, or given the death sentence for a minor offense, think of this like skipping all your doctor appointments for a few years and then suddenly learning you've got a terminal illness.

My boss and I had a happy honeymoon in my first weeks and months on this job. But once our professional nuptials graduated into normal work patterns and habits, tension began to build. I sensed there was something about my personality she wasn't liking. I didn't know what I might have been doing wrong. And she wasn't saying.

I realized much too late where I had committed what seemed like a tiny misdemeanor—one that was never fully resolved. My boss was fond of documenting every working project in emails with the full team cc'd. I thought I was doing the right thing by following in her footsteps. I had long-standing professional and personal relationships with her two bosses that predated all of us working at this company. In one of my emails to my boss, I cc'd our entire team, as she always did, including her two bosses. Big mistake. She got pissed. I was told not to cc her bosses. There's an old song called, "Things That Make You Go Hmmmm." I took the slap on the wrist and moved on, but I missed the deeper clues about the power dynamics in the relationship with my boss. I stayed secretly angry at her passive-aggressive attitude. And she likely never trusted me again.

Looking back, I could have been the one to break the iceberg before it was too late. It didn't occur to me that she remained pissed for almost a year over what I thought was something so small. I can see now that she may have felt threatened by my prior relationship to her bosses, and I should've found a way to let her know that I wasn't gunning for her job. I missed the chance to build trust and that did me in.

Here's the lesson: Make sure there's an open line of communication with the people you're working for. Get over any fear to ask, "How am I doing?" when you get the feeling something starts to go sideways. (Oh, and don't cc your boss's boss on any internal communication!)

If you're in the boss chair next time, let your team know that whenever they think something has gone off the rails, they can and should take the initiative to talk with you. You'll earn more loyalty and better performance from every employee who knows they have open access to you for these check-ins. As a boss, you can remove the fear that keeps your people from doing their best work.

Welcome to the Jungle

It's hard to believe how far we've evolved as a species if you fell victim to people who behave like animals on the job. A bad economy and a troubled work environment can turn coworkers into predators or prey. "Survival of the fittest" doesn't appear on top of most job descriptions, but it could. I'm sorry for any attacks you suffered during your last time in the jungle. Wild creatures most commonly encountered include Backstabbers, Gossipmongers, Entitled Babies, Credit Hogs, Silent Sheep,

Thirsty Vampires, Raging Bulls, and Poisonous Snakes. Beware of all these beasts as you do the research and homework to find your next, best job. And do not feed the animals.

Early in my career, I was warned that working inside a big company environment meant accepting the fact that doing your actual job happens only about 50 percent of the time. The remaining time can be spent communicating about doing that job—with your boss, your employees, and your coworkers. Managing up and down the company ladder is half the battle. It hurts to say this, but office politics is often half the job.

Anytime you've been taken advantage of by somebody climbing over you to better their own position, you get another psychic scar. But that scar is a reminder to recognize similar warning signs when you meet new teammates.

Once you are out of the jungle you still need to beware of Gossipmongers. Wasting time here can turn into a guilty pleasure. It's petty poison when you're on the job, but it can be one of your most dangerous habits when you're stuck out of work. Try not to turn into an amateur conspiracy theorist, concocting and sharing elaborate reasons for your downfall. You need every ounce of that brain power focused on what you need to do next. It's not a good look. Anytime you give safe harbor to someone who gets off on running around the rumor mill is time you could have spent creating something productive.

"Don't Do Me Like That"

Your friends prefer you when you're not constantly complaining about every single detail of struggle you're experiencing in your career. This is a hard truth to swallow. Looking back, it took me too many years to accept this. I used to carry the weight of every career battle, and carelessly dump that heavy load on every friend who would listen. (My crisis is also their emergency, right?) I was behaving like a character in an old black-and-white World War II movie: a radio reporter, on the roof of a building with bombs dropping all around me, broadcasting live to all the ships at sea and every friend and relative who could hear my voice from inside the comfort of their own homes. My audio was interrupted constantly by sounds of gunfire and screaming in the background. We take you now to the sounds of this battlefield broadcast:

I'm not sure if you're going to be able to hear my voice!

I couldn't let this horrible event pass without broadcasting all the gory details of the carnage taking place around me.

I've just come back from a meeting with the HR department where I learned that our division is being restructured. Most of my team was just eliminated. [Screeching sounds of rocket fire in the background] . . . I get to keep my job, for now. But get this . . . a new vice president has just been hired to run the sales team and she starts Monday with everyone who used to report to our boss, the senior VP, now reporting to this new VP. [More gunfire can be heard close by.]

I just looked her up. She looks like she's got to be at least fifteen years younger than me and I don't see anything on her LinkedIn that can explain how she has enough experience to get this job. [The sound of an explosion in the distance.]

At this moment, the broadcast cuts off suddenly. I've lost all communication. [My cell battery died.] I'd like to think the audience is terrified that the worst has happened. I imagine every listener frantically trying to reestablish contact to make sure I had not just been taken out by sniper fire.

But the opposite is true. The audience of friends and relatives back home are unbelievably busy going about their own lives with just as many challenges as I'm experiencing. The abrupt end of my broadcast may have secretly been a great relief for an audience forced to listen to another rant from the battlefield.

I was guilty of making countless broadcasts like this to all my friends during private job wars in the past. I made the bad assumption that my friends needed every painful detail of troubles at work. I used to complain too much about work with my family. It wasn't fair. Bad communication and disrespect at work isn't the kind of behavior you want to bring home to your personal life.

It's better to ask for help and a calm conversation, than it is to assume it's acceptable to turn on a firehose of pain, without realizing it may be driving the people who love you mad.

Keep the Edge, Lose the Chip

That chip on your shoulder has to go. I used to get overly annoyed at all the wrongs I felt people were doing "to me" on the job. I thought that steam was fuel in my professional gas tank that added an edge needed to succeed. The older I got, the more I realized those grievances were slowing me down, and not allowing for a smoother ride. More reflection revealed that my secret chip was a lot more visible to other people than I realized.

The will to keep striving for success works best when you flick that chip off your shoulder and keep the edge and fire in your belly for more positive motivation. If you're secretly pissed half the time, or outwardly blaming other people for every misstep, that energy gets in the way of finding the right solutions to your search.

We Meet Again

Depending on the size of your industry, there's always a chance that people you've had serious conflicts with in the past will pop back up in later chapters in your career. You'll be much better prepared to handle the shock of meeting a former rival as a new coworker if you heal past conflicts internally and find ways to make amends, if possible, with people you've clashed with before. I can't lie. I have a small black list. But anytime I've been able to mend old wounds with workmates and even bosses is a chance to be a slightly more evolved human. You always want as many positive recommendations as possible when you're out of work. Anyone who may be bad-mouthing you is a problem you want to solve, if you can. Some of these past relationships may be too broken to be repaired, but you'll go a long way toward removing your own inner demons if you try.

Crossing the Line

In the last few years, many company heads have been removed after allegations came to light about their abusive behaviors. This is not a tell-all book, but I've worked for a number of senior executives who were proven to be responsible for hurting employees they were managing. Some of these monsters who were terminated for heinous acts in the workplace were very public figures. Media coverage of those cases heightened the level of awareness and intolerance for abuse. Corporations and leaders who had looked the other way for far too long are finally paying closer attention and investigating every allegation of harm.

If you are still on the job and are being discriminated against, or abused in any way, please seek the help you need from the human resources team. Elevate the problem to your senior management right away. If you just lost your job and suffered abuse that has still not been resolved, please get the professional counsel you need, psychological and legal, to make sure you're safe, and to protect your rights.

If you lost a job because *you* were accused of any harmful actions, please talk this out with friends you trust and reach out for professional help too. Future companies will check your background and references before they offer you a job. As a headhunter, I work with candidates on every issue that rose to the level of an HR incident in previous positions. When you attempt to cover up these problems, you run a high risk the truth will come out.

If you're asked about any past conflicts and you sound evasive, or you're not taking enough responsibility for your role in what went down, that red flag will most likely prevent you from getting hired. On the other hand, if you deal directly and openly with any serious past HR concerns that could come up during a job interview, you have an opportunity to prove that you're straightforward, humble, and willing to take responsibility for the conflict and any role you played in the situation. Time is up for BS. Do your best to carefully rehearse a concise explanation of any serious issue. If you had fault, let the interviewer know what you've done to correct the problem. Summon the bravery to address these incidents with the integrity required to earn trust from the person you need to hire you now.

Death by Email

The best advice you'll ever get about email in work and in life is to never write and send a message that will put you in jeopardy if it was read by everyone in the world. Any angry or inappropriate email can and will be used against you in a court of law or public opinion—and by every person you wrote who feels that you crossed the line of decency and professionalism. This remains true even after you've written a risky email, decided not to send it, and deleted it. A smart friend once made this point very clear by warning "there's no such thing as delete." Your message is sitting on a server that somebody with the right technical skills can access anytime.

Do yourself and everyone you ever exchange emails with a major favor by working harder to keep all communication to the fewest words possible. This isn't just about fear of reprisal, or being taken out of context. Learning to be more direct and succinct brings you better results and respect. Work harder to remove all the setup from what you're about to say. Just say it.

End on a High Note

Not every work environment is fraught with minefields, and every day in the office does not have to feel like you're working in an active battleground. But be ready for all the challenges that will come at you next time. Look for the kind of management and team that has the maximum potential for much less psychodrama than you may have suffered in the past.

When I was in my mid-thirties, I was extremely lucky to have a manager who made our mission and goals clear. Mike was the kind of leader who didn't keep moving the goalposts, making it impossible to win. Mike didn't run a "nothing is ever good enough" environment. This outstanding leader regularly gave our team support, feedback, and rewards for a job well done. Instead of the usual level of stress and unrealistic expectations, this boss made it his business to make sure we could do our business without any unnecessary drama.

Our fearless leader wasn't quite as lucky with his own boss. However, if he was reamed out by the head of the company, he'd walk back down the hall to his direct reports and prevent shit from flowing downstream. Mike didn't take the heat out on us. We'd all come up with achievable solutions on what he needed to take back down to the corner office as the remedy.

Mike's way is the way to be. If you're a manager, be more like Mike. If you're getting ready to interview for your next, best job, do everything you can to find managers who are open-minded, clear communicators. And no matter where you land next, promise yourself that you're going to do a better job communicating regularly and reasonably to avoid and resolve conflicts before it all goes too far.

And . . . Breathe

You just survived the first three chapters, looking back on the pain and lessons learned from losing your job. The hardest workplace challenges produce battle scars, but they also produce wisdom to get you ready to rise up and win what's next. I hope you'll work with the strategies that make you stronger, to heal the anger, lose the chip on your shoulder, keep the edge, and repair the wrongs you may have done to the people you've worked with.

Remember that it's *not* "just business." This is all extremely personal. Job loss is a major life event and a true threat to your sanity that needs to be healed before you can create what's next. Try not to work on these first three chapters alone. Call friends who've already told you they felt bad about your situation and offered help. You've now got a new way for them to step up if they have a few hours to dissect the past and prep the future. And it's much easier than asking to borrow money. (But I'm not ruling that out. I've borrowed in emergencies and will offer a loan whenever I can to a friend in trouble.) Work through the 11 Survival Steps in chapter 2 and the chapter 3 strategies to heal your emotions and crank up your logic. The only way to actually accomplish *all* this—and receive the benefits of all the strategies—is to *calendarize* the work you need to do now in your daily job search. Now, let's drive North.

CHAPTER 4

Your North Star

While I was working at VH1 in the late '90s, I had the honor of spending one of the greatest days of my life with George Harrison. He'd been traveling with Ravi Shankar and Ravi's wife Sukanya to promote the new album George had just produced for his friend and mentor—and came to our studio as a surprise guest. During the interview, while surrounded by a tiny crew, a few of our friends, and his son Dhani, George performed a new, not-yet-released song for us called "Any Road." This once-in-a-lifetime session stays vivid in my mind and heart to this day. His simple message in this song is a profound gift to all of us from my favorite Beatle, and a worthy spiritual compass. You can't just take "any road" to find where you need to be.

So where do you want to go? What do you want to do next? You need to determine your destination before you can figure out how to get there. I've heard too many jobseekers say they're "willing to take anything." They believe they'd be lucky to get any job, and beggars can't be choosers. Don't fall into that defeatist way of thinking. Don't give away your power. Your last boss may have stripped away your job, salary, and health care, but nobody robbed you of your ability to make your own decisions.

About ten years after my day with George, I found myself on another road. This famous, 5.6-mile stretch of land is in Northern California, where many of the world's most game-changing ideas and companies have been founded and financed by the tech-savvy investment firms of Silicon Valley. Venture capitalists' offices on Sand Hill Road run through Palo Alto, Menlo Park, and Woodside, California. In the VC world, this road is hallowed ground.

My visits to this legendary real estate were about seeking capital for a new business I'd created called My Damn Channel. My team and I had built one of the world's first original online studios and networks to produce and distribute digital video series—many years before Netflix and Amazon joined the race.

I never got quite enough cash from Sand Hill Road, but every visit to one of these jaw-droppingly elegant conference rooms began with an offer for a free bottle of water and ended with priceless advice about business from brilliant investors. The most important counsel imparted to me on one of these visits was to do one thing, above all else, well: Focus. I was told that the formula for success included a commandment to concentrate on doing only one thing better than any competitor. If, and (only) when, you're beating your competition with repeatable revenues, profits, brand clarity, and customer loyalty should you consider expanding that focus and branching off on to other avenues to explore what else your business can offer the marketplace.

Take the advice of George Harrison and the minds behind some of the most successful companies on earth. Don't take any road to find any job. You can succeed if you focus. You can win your next, best job much more quickly if you decide which road you're going to take in your career. This focus is your North Star—your guiding purpose and passion that will lead you to exactly where you need to be. The minute you can see your own North Star is the minute every decision about where you should be working and with whom becomes clear.

We all witnessed enough pain and loss during the global pandemic to be asking ourselves deeper questions about what's most important in our lives and careers. When the world came to a grinding halt, days felt like months, and months felt like years locked inside our homes. If you're one of the tens of millions of people who lost a job during this crisis, my hope is that you grew hungry for more than just any job next time around. My hope is that you found inspiration to want to find the right job.

If you lost people you love to the virus, my heart is with you. Time is one way to heal the pain of loss. Purpose is an even more powerful antidote to pain. Finding the next, best job is a noble quest. Winning meaningful work can restore the passion and power you lost. I'm going to offer you a map. This is a journey from your heart to your head, and from your head back into the workforce.

No Direction Home

On the twenty-fourth day of May, in a galaxy far, far away, I was busy being born on Bob Dylan's birthday. Bob is the patron saint of self-creation. He invented who he wanted to be. And he's reinvented that idea as many times as he felt the need. If the Wizard of Oz were here right now, hanging with you, me, and Dylan, he'd tell us that we all have the exact same power to reinvent who we need to be next.

There's nothing stopping you—unless you want to throw cold water on every idea by asking the opinion of everyone you know. I found a recorded conversation with Bob Dylan from the early '80s that always holds a place in my heart. This conversation took place late at night in a New York City hotel. In response to a question about people trying to tell Bob how to make his music, Dylan replied:

> Oh . . . there's always people trying to tell you how to do everything in your life. If you really don't know what to do and you don't care what to do, then just ask somebody's opinion. You'll get a million different opinions. If you don't want to do something, ask someone's opinion and they'll just verify it for you. The easiest way to do something is to just not ask anybody's opinion.

I mean if you really believe in what you're doing . . . I've just asked people's opinion and it's been a great mistake, in different areas. Yeah, you know what's right. When those things come you know what's right. A lot of times you might be farming around and not knowing what's right and you might do something dumb, but that's only because you don't know what to do in the first place. But if you know what's right and it strikes you at a certain time then you can usually believe that instinct. And if you act on it, then you'll be successful at it. Whatever it is.

When you launch your job search, it can be dangerous to ask for too many opinions. You can be lured into chasing every potential shiny object. And whenever you follow someone else's path, eventually you're going to find out you've been heading in the wrong direction toward a destination you never wanted in the first place.

Name That Tune

Nothing makes clear sense when you're stuck, until the moment you decide what's next. If you don't choose, you lose valuable time. You may lose the job you should have won because you were taking too long to find out what your best path should be. I've learned from talking to thousands of people on both sides of the hiring table that the number one reason people get stuck in between jobs, again (#iBJA) is their lack of ability to focus on the right, specific job path.

This land of indecision can be deadly. No matter how competitive the hiring process may be, no matter how much unemployment is out there, and no matter how long you've been out of work, the biggest barrier to breaking your bad streak is fixable right now. When you pick a direction and "name that tune," you can start singing to every target company who wants to hear your song.

Imagine a swimming pool with six different lanes. Each lane represents a specific career choice. You may have credible reasons for believing you're perfectly capable of swimming in each one of these six different lanes. But you can only swim in one lane at a time. Pick a lane. If you spend your whole job search shifting lanes, you'll only commit one-sixth of the time you should be swimming in any one lane. With this strategy it'll take too long to reach the other side. And that's where your next, best job is waiting. By picking a lane, and staying in it, swimming as smart and strong as you can, you get to the finish line much faster. The power of your focus will yield better results than continuing to change your mind about exactly what kind of work you should be pursuing. You can determine the best long-term strategy for your career. Cue the music.

"INCOMING!"

The greatest single night of my lucky professional life happened on a small stage in a tiny rock club in Worcester, Massachusetts, in 1981. I was working as a rock DJ and music director at a radio station called WAAF. At the ripe old age of twenty-one, I proved that anything is possible if you ask. I found a way to meet and interview Mick Jagger, and over the course of a few weeks I convinced the Rolling Stones to play a private club gig for the fans of my radio station. WAAF made rock history when I put this show together with the Stones. Superhuman experiences are possible if you're crazy enough to believe you can do anything you set your mind to.

Years later, I got to work with the Stones again and asked Keith Richards if being fearless was part of what enabled him to realize his dream of becoming a working musician. He said that, for him, it was less about fear and more about the fact that he only knew how to be the exact person he wanted to be. He knew that to be anything less than who he was would be a lie. A beautiful soul breathes through Keith. His talent is surrounded by joy, confidence, mastery, mystery, magic, nonstop energy, long-term vision, comrades, community, and unique riffs that he channels from the great beyond through his guitar.

We can't all be Keith. But we can all take two notes from his playbook and apply his magic to our own careers. Keith not only figured out who he wanted to be, he always stuck to his guns, without fail. He found a way to trust his instincts about what to do next whenever he was stuck creatively.

I heard the following story about Keith from Don Was. Don is one of the best musicians, record producers, and musical divining rods I've ever worked with. I have the honor of calling Don a friend and collaborator. Don has produced countless musical heroes and innovators, including all the albums by the Rolling Stones since the early '90s. When Don works with the Stones, it can take more than a few days for all of the men to show up in the same room at the same time. With all the masters in attendance, there's never any guarantee their labor will birth new creations worthy of making it to vinyl. Don said that after years of working with the band, he always knew something important was about to happen when he saw Keith Richards make one consistent gesture and invoke one sacred word.

The minute Keith detected what could be a new legendary lick, he would thrust his right hand high up toward the sky. He'd extend his twisted, bony index finger to the gods and shout: "INCOMING!" And a new riff struck like lightning.

The moment an inspired idea hits you is magic to be respected. You don't have to be a Rolling Stone to put your finger up to the sky and invoke lightning to find purpose. I wish you the same thing I wish for my son and two daughters: that you find these moments, the "incoming" messages that hand you pure inspiration to know what you want to do. If you didn't think the world needed you to do that now more than ever, it does.

The Burning Passion of Pirates

One of the hardest things about having a long career is that you can get further and further away from the "burning passion of the pirate." I woke up one morning to record my daily video on job searching and remembered a younger, wilder sense of adventure, a time when I would leap across the sea and chase the next dream. Think back on some of your wildest dreams. What were the first ideas about what you wanted to become when you grew up? We've all got a little pirate spirit buried in our childhood memories. See if you can tap into that and remember those feelings when you were first inspired to want to be "somebody." Imagine your sword outstretched, when you first saw an opening in the world and secretly proclaimed, "Let me in!" Recapturing that passion and deciding to move toward what might thrill you is not the worthless dream of a child. You can create a grown-up plan to turn dreams into reality and find work that lights a fire inside your soul.

One of the greatest spiritual gifts I ever received came from an enlightened and generous friend named Franci. She dedicated her life to helping people learn how to paint better pictures. Franci Prowse was one of the first people who taught me to visualize what and where I needed to be. She encouraged all her students to paint better pictures by doing a powerful mental exercise. "Decide what you want, need, and will be doing in the future," she'd tell us. "Now, imagine it, in fine detail. Now, picture it happening today, in the present moment. What do you see in your surroundings? What are you wearing? Where are you seated? How does it feel to be doing the work you were meant to be doing?" When you experience an imagined future, you've already started to create the reality. Even if the most logical, practical parts of you are screaming ("I just need a damn pay-check!"), stick with me and ask that voice to pipe down and believe that cash is right in your hand. You need your confidence back.

What you want to do next is already in your mind and heart. I hope you have someone like Franci in your life to help you visualize and create what you need. My Franci is on the other side, watching over this book right now and cheering you on to find your North Star.

What Exactly Is the North Star?

Hiring managers only give a fast, initial look at candidates online. Branding yourself with a clear North Star in the headline of your résumé and LinkedIn profile defines the role that best reflects your passion, expertise, and experience. If you don't know how to come up with the best title, you're about to follow a map to find True North. Once you capture the clarity about the work you should be doing, you're on a trajectory that will serve you forever.

Your North Star is your long-term professional identity. It's the first impression, defining exactly what you have to offer in the workplace. I've seen too many people take an opposite approach by listing a garden variety of different job titles on top of their LinkedIn profile and résumé. Many headhunters and CV (curriculum vitae) writers advise you to be more things to more people to increase your odds at being hired. This approach clouds the focus your next boss needs to see.

Once you name your North Star, this declaration of who you are professionally will increase your success in finding the right job more than anything else you'll read in this book.

Butcher, Baker, Candlestick Maker

"I'm a storyteller. I'm a brand builder. I'm a marketer. I'm experienced. I'm a senior executive." None of these descriptions are the correct choice to display on the top of your LinkedIn or résumé. They may describe credibility, but they're not job titles. You need a bull's-eye. A direct hit. In the fewest consonants and vowels possible, you need to claim your future with a specific job title that actually exists in a business. If you're a marketer, what kind? Specificity equals victory. Ambiguous and generic lose.

I know most of my fellow headhunters, recruiters, and job-getting experts suggest showing multiple job titles on your professional résumé to cast the widest net. And most job seekers think like this: "If I can't pay the bills . . . if I'm sinking . . . if there are millions of other people out of work . . . then I have to increase my odds of getting hired by showing as many different versions of my professional self as I can." That's not the right strategy. Hiring managers are seeking candidates with as much specific experience as possible for the exact job they are trying to fill. In order to increase your odds, you've got to perfectly position yourself as the person who most clearly meets all the requirements and qualifications of the job description.

If a company is looking to hire a butcher, saying you're a butcher, a baker, and a candlestick maker doesn't give you a leg up. Quite the opposite. You will be three times less likely to be hired if you tell everyone that you're

83

seeking three different jobs. The company seeking a new butcher wants the candidate with the most experience in meat. All the candidates who feel like they have to show their baking skills and wax-shaping mastery along with butcher bona fides are headed to the bottom of the résumé pile. Hiring execs want specialists—not generalists. Don't be a Swiss Army knife.

When you reclaim your professional identity and choose the right career and the perfect job title, your decision brings clarity, and that clarity is contagious. Everyone in your personal and professional networks can finally help you much more than before by making the best connections for you at the right target companies because they have a clear understanding of what job you're seeking.

Here's a sad truth—and another reason to focus: Many of your friends are too busy to figure this all out for you. Although they love you, they may not necessarily have 100 percent of the knowledge about every detail that should be influencing your decisions about how to find the right job. If you focus clearly on what you need next, and communicate that exact job title you're seeking to the people who care about you most, it becomes massively easier for all of them to help you search and win.

Finding Your True North

LinkedIn never used to be as tough as Tinder. Nonstop surfing of job sites can make you feel adrift in an endless sea of humanity, hopelessly lookin' for love. If you upload a résumé and your profile doesn't pop perfectly for a hiring manager in the blink of an eye, they swipe away in an instant. The game is lost before you've even had a chance to make your first move with a cover letter or an interview.

Recruiters and headhunters don't have time to study everything you want to communicate about yourself in their first quick look at your digital profile. These people are under their own tremendous pressures to fill jobs with the best candidates in the shortest time. Too many résumés are submitted for every one of the most desirable jobs. The people looking to hire you suffer from the same cultural obsessions with instant gratification and digital multitasking that you do. How often do you skim instead of read, patiently? You may even be doing it now. In today's job-hunting jungle, you need to present a sharply honed, succinct first look at who you are— in the most compelling way possible on your LinkedIn, your résumé, or CV. We are going to rip these all apart and rebuild them in chapter 5. But not until we help you define your true North Star first. Here are examples of the wrong ways to describe yourself professionally on your résumé or LinkedIn profile:

- Business Development / Content Creation / Management

- Rainmaker / Revenue Generator

- Seeking my next career opportunity

- Digital Consigliere

- Storyteller

- Creative People Person

- Marketing Guru

- Thought Leader

- Freelancer

- Consultant

- Looking for my next challenge

- Experienced professional, passionate, dedicated, driven to succeed

These are all nonstarters. Your North Star needs to state your professional brand in the fewest words. The answer to anyone asking what you do should be as clear as saying you're a publicist, or a plumber, or a personal trainer. Anything less specific, or any multiple choice answers, dilutes the point and reduces the clarity you need to get hired.

Star Points

Here are the three points leading to your North Star.

Star Point 1—The Next Best Job in Your Heart

Tom Petty once said, "Do something you really like, and hopefully it pays the rent. As far as I'm concerned, that's success." From the time I was very young, I was lucky to have an uncommon idea planted in my mind. I thought it was completely acceptable to have a career that connects with your passions. I never subscribed to the view that said we should stuff our working life into the un-fun bucket for most of our waking hours, and keep joy and pleasure waiting somewhere off in the wings as rare rewards.

The journey to find your North Star begins in the heart, before you travel to your head. You can feel what's in your heart much more easily if you release the negative energy you experienced on the last job. (So I hope you've read through chapter 3 carefully. If not, go back and do it.) The people who may have hurt you in the past are not coming along for the ride to what's next. Take an imaginary swig of some psychic mouthwash to rinse all that bad taste out of your mouth—and get on with today's work.

Another way to get out of an angst-filled headspace—and into a more creative and productive mind-set—is to ignite the positive parts of the brain with visualization exercises. Imagine you've just won the lottery. Fifty million dollars lands in your lap. If you now have more in the bank than you've ever dreamed, what would you do for work? What would the most creative, productive job be now? What's the secret career you always wanted but never thought you deserved? If you put all the fear and worry aside, and allow yourself to believe you can have any job in the world, your better angels might start singing. These are the voices you can never hear if you're drowning them all out with a noise-shouting *No!* You need the power of *Yes* back in your life. And this power does not cost $50 million to capture. The exact price is zero dollars.

This exercise is no different from me deciding I want to get a toasted Everything Bagel with cream cheese at my friendly nearby bagel store. I'm a Jew from Brooklyn. If it's Sunday, I neeeeeed that bagel. I can smell the freshly baked bread, I can feel the crunch of that first bite between my teeth, the moment I make the decision to get one. I have not yet left the house. I haven't even gotten up from my chair. But I can taste it. The same goes for your dream job. All you need to do is see, hear, and feel what your heart might want if there was absolutely no chance of rejection or failure.

Invite the pain and fear of what you've lost to step aside. If you replace self-limiting thoughts with the biggest ideas about your perfect, future job, then you've just released the energy to turn those thoughts into reality. It's that simple. This is a power and a creative skill you can call upon every day. From a place of perfect imagination, your search for a new North Star comes into sharper focus.

Take your heart out for a freedom ride. Clear off your desk, turn off the phone, shut the door, and take a few minutes just for you. Make believe you woke up one morning and found the entire world asleep. Imagine you had complete power to claim any job you want. Imagine a perfect job, an inspired company, unlimited resources, salary up the wazoo, a beautiful office. This job answers all your hopes and dreams. And when the whole world wakes up, nobody can take this away.

What job did you see yourself doing?

Make a list of all the best jobs that come to your heart, not your head. Think about this list like a long overdue love letter to yourself. I won't write an entire chapter on the rules of brainstorming. That's why God made the internet. But go get a six-foot whiteboard and your favorite color markers, or an oversized drawing pad, crayons, paint brushes, your most precise ballpoint, or your writing weapon of choice.

A true brainstorm should start with a ton of ideas and no edits. Keep writing ideas in a completely judgment-free zone. Don't hesitate to write down something that might look dumb. Don't talk yourself out of anything. Go for volume. Write down as many ideas as you can. Do not allow the "No" Police to barge into your lovely head. Don't let one ounce of pessimism seep in. Reject realism. Embrace the future. These are the jobs you really want. Stay in this imagination zone.

A few jobs on your brainstorm list may date back to your earliest childhood dreams—from that pirate spirit. Imagine reclaiming one of those favorite fantasies when everything was in front of you, without all the stress. Your passion, imagination, and the fire inside don't have an expiration date. The world sometimes makes it harder to believe you can be who you want to be. I believe you can decide—right now.

We're about to introduce logic into the equation. Study the list of jobs in your heart and see if you can narrow them down to a tighter list of favorites. Even if you have the one true answer already whispering in your ear, prioritize all the ideas you listed for "Star Point 1—The Next Best Job in Your Heart" into your Top 3.

Star Point 2— The Next, Best Job in Your Head

The second step of the process in naming your North Star calls for a journey from your heart to your head. It's time to think about the real world and plant your feet firmly on the ground. What are you good at? What training do you have? What mountains have you already climbed and what are the skills that got you there? The mix of what you want to do most and what you know you can do best is what's going to lead you in the right direction.

Here are key questions to find out if you can match up the list you just made from the heart with the list you're about to make from your logical mind and you'll have two-thirds of the answer to what your next best job should be:

- Does every job you're dreaming about line up with the work you do best?

- What are your strongest work skills and superpowers?

- What was your most successful job to date—
  where you achieved the best results, the highest
  performance reviews, and your most job
  satisfaction?

- What would the people you worked for, and
  teammates you worked with, say about you? (If
  we shot them all full of truth serum, what would
  they say?)

Zero in on all these answers by reviewing your current
résumé. Start at the bottom with your very first job and
work your way up to the most recent gig. Identify the
work you did that hit big and mattered most. When you
find those highpoints, you can start to see a pattern.
This review can help solidify the best option for the work
you know you can do best.

But here comes a problem. If the best job in your
heart (Star Point 1) doesn't match up with the next job
in your head (Star Point 2), you're likely finding a gap in
the experience you need to win. Can you pivot from the
work that you've been doing to the work that you want?

CAN I PIVOT?

The quick answer is yes, you can pivot. The more specific answer is: not too far. We all know what it feels like
to pretend we're the best person for a job we know we're
not really qualified for. Raise your hand if you've ever
applied for a position that you were not perfectly qualified
to fill. Endless online surfing and uploading applications

to random job postings is a surefire joy killer, and a losing strategy. In moments of weakness, it's reasonable to want to attempt anything to end the angst of being out of work. But don't throw valuable energy at whatever oddball options happen to show up. Every résumé you submit that doesn't line up with the requirements listed on the job description is a waste of time.

Too many job seekers hang on to an imaginary two-word lifeline tied to a false sense of confidence. They say, "I have *transferable skills*." Try to understand why this logic will not convince hiring managers you're the right person. When someone's sink is clogged and they are looking for a plumber, they know exactly what they need and they need it now. They're not going to hire someone who could maybe, sort of, do the job, eventually.

So how do you pivot? How do you connect the dots from where you've been to where you want to be? If you have a work history with a number of previous jobs, you've likely had to pivot to some extent already. Whether you want to pivot within the same field, or you want to pivot to a better field of dreams, your story needs to be told clearly and credibly on the résumé and during the interviews.

Here's an example about pivoting from a session with one of my clients: Helen started her career after college as an assistant in the social media marketing department of a children's clothing brand. One of her oldest friends worked in the fashion business and she had the right connections to land the job. This entry-level position gave Helen solid initial experience, but her boss was let go after only a year so she was out of a job too. A search for jobs in other clothing companies wasn't working, and then she was offered a job when another friend helped her get an interview at a real estate firm. Even though this new gig took Helen out of fashion where she preferred to be, it was time to pay the bills. And the hiring manager at the real estate firm needed someone to support their social media marketing team. This pivot wasn't the perfect move on Helen's desired path, but now her career track had two back-to-back positions pointing to her North Star as a social media marketer.

Star Point 3—Proving It

What you'd love to do most and what you're convinced you do best can only lead to your next, best job if you have enough past accomplishments to prove you're qualified for the position. What you feel in your heart and know in your head need to be reinforced by the evidence that you've done this work multiple times—and recently. Your North Star burns brightest when you can back up the career goal with credibility, repetition, and recency on your résumé and LinkedIn profile.

In chapter 5, you'll get the tools and strategies to successfully market your professional brand with a new LinkedIn profile and résumé. But you need essential preparation first to prove the third point of your North Star before rewriting your entire work history in a more effective way. You can't tell lies about your background, but you need to learn how to shape your story to create the most organized and cohesive presentation. Star Point 3 focuses on the "greatest hits" and specific accomplishments from past jobs that line up best with your new Star Points 1 and 2.

I know you may be wondering what happens if your job history doesn't have a straight trajectory. What if the job you had from 2014 to 2018 was definitely consistent with your North Star, but from 2018 to 2019, you had to take a thankless job that had nothing to do with your real career before getting back on the right track in 2020?

Our résumé and LinkedIn job seeking clients have the years listed for all their past employment, but we drop the months. Here's how a client's revised history reads:

2014–2018:   Past Job consistent with the North Star

~~2018–2019:   store manager off main career track~~
[This comes out]

2019–2021:   Most Recent Job consistent with
North Star

When the job you want most in your heart (Star Point 1) is consistent with your recent job history in similar positions that you've held at least more than once before (Star Point 2), and you have specific achievements in those past jobs to prove your case (Star Point 3), then you found the clarity to name and claim your North

Star. Once this decision is made, your job search can move from a crawl to warp speed.

Sometimes the path isn't obvious. Take my own LinkedIn profile, right before finding a new North Star as a headhunter. My heart was telling me to find a new position that would devote all my time to helping people. This ex-audiobook, ex–online video pro, ex-Radiohead, ex-TV, and ex-etcetera could be seen as too confusing without a new narrative focus that clearly pointed in a singular direction. I had credible evidence that I had been hiring the right people for the right jobs in all my previous positions. This was the organizing principle that gave me a new way to tell my story. I had the experience needed for my company clients and my job candidates to trust that I could do this new job as a headhunter.

I was completely stuck until I made this decision to claim a new North Star, to rewrite my own work history, and to market myself (chapter 5).

Here's the first part of the book you may not like: If the job of your heart is one that you haven't done before, recently and repeatedly, you're not going to be hired for that position. Sorry for dumping ice cold water on you, but patience is a virtue, grasshopper. You *can* have the job of your heart at a more junior level than you thought you were ready to tackle. (Follow "The Straight Line Theory" in chapter 8.) Getting in where you want to be at any level is the far better strategy than continuing to hold out for the most senior roles if your current job search is taking too long. We're going to talk more about leverage and the best strategies to negotiate a new deal and close like a pro in chapter 10.

ET: Entrepreneur's 'Tude

I'm always surprised how few people decide to choose the path of an entrepreneur. After weighing the pros and cons of working for someone else vs. working for yourself, almost 99 percent of the people I counsel think it's much harder to go out on your own. Only 1 percent have decided they will be more fulfilled on the path as an entrepreneur. These special clients have what I call an *entrepreneur's 'tude,* and it's an attitude you may want to adopt, even if you've decided you're better off working in a company run by someone that isn't you.

Imagine being completely comfortable with the fact that no matter how perfect any business plan looks in black and white, conditions will change. Some changes can be easily handled and controlled. But here's a terrifying thought for all of the control freaks in the house: Some changes will throw everything totally out of whack. I know, you may need a minute and a glass of water. Are you okay? All right. Let's continue.

An entrepreneur's 'tude constantly builds muscles designed to withstand change. These are smart muscles. They know the walls could fall down at any time. They know the boss is going to be toppled at some point. Entrepreneur's 'tude builds brainpower to consider the larger financial world outside the four walls of the one company you're working in at any given time. That world includes competition that should be watched like a multi-dimensional chessboard. The larger view of an entrepreneur is always focused on national and global economic trends that could impact the success and survival of their current company.

There's great heart and strength of conviction inside every true entrepreneur. There's fiery passion for the final product and the entire process it takes to get there. Entrepreneurs always act like they're protecting their own child. You wouldn't recklessly abandon someone you love, would you?

Here's where you might call me a hopeless romantic, idealist, dreamer. You're missing out on the beauty of your working life by not listening to your own voice, and following your North Star, with an entrepreneur's 'tude—even if you work for someone else. An ownership mind-set for every project you handle is magnetic inspiration. People love being around someone who doesn't panic every time there's change. Entrepreneurs are famous for having a B plan, a C plan and a D plan, because failure is never an option. This 'tude will serve you well in a constantly changing job market. You need to look a little further into the future to make sure you have backup plans for a steady paycheck.

And if you do have the entrepreneurial bug? Maybe that's something you should explore. Is starting your own business risky? Sure. Is starting a business a ton of work? Absolutely. But if that is the dream humming in your heart, don't stifle it.

I know it's a big decision, but here is a baby step to get you started. My dad used to simplify every major career decision with an ancient personal device called a yellow legal pad. When I was a kid, Dad acted like a yellow pad held the keys to the universe. Of course you'll need a pen. Mike says, "Get me a pen!" (I promised my best friend Mike I'd put that in my first book, and there's absolutely no way I'm allowing my editor or my publisher to delete this secret coded message of love.)

Now take that pen and that yellow pad and draw one straight vertical line right down the middle. Title the column on the left side YES and the column on the right side NO. On the left, list all the ideas that would make being an entrepreneur the next, best job of your life. On the right, list all the reasons why you believe this may not be the best option:

YES	NO
• I can finally do the work I wanted to do most.	• How will I afford health care?
• I can set my own hours.	• I've never been good enough at business.
• I'll never get fired.	• It's going to be too hard to get clients.
• I can work from home.	• I'm not good at marketing myself.
• I'll never commute again.	• I work better in a structured environment.
• I don't need an outside office or any of the expense.	• I'm not good enough at deadlines.
• I can live anywhere in the world and still work.	• I don't have enough confidence.
	• Who's going to do any of the legal work I need?
• I won't have to spend hundreds of hours a year worrying about what to wear.	• I suck at accounting.
	• I've never done this before.
	• What if it doesn't work?

My father's method of simply writing down all the pros and cons of a decision like this almost forces you to study the No list and concentrate on how to solve the potential problems holding you back. Dad's advice was to find the people you need to deliver what you're missing. Turn the page and make a new list of all the professional people you know who can play the right positions on your team.

- Accountant

- Lawyer

- Publicity and Marketing

- Sales Reps

There's a myth about entrepreneurs being independent. The only way to be successful is to be interdependent on the smartest people you respect and trust and who can inspire you to do your best work together. You can't win without a crazy mystical concept called "trusting people." If you decide to start a business of your own, you'll likely need to form a founders' team of like-minded pros who are all committed to the new company vision. Even if you don't have any start-up money to launch a business, you will have one priceless resource: your word. When you form agreements and sign contracts with cofounders who rally around your vision, you decide the exact roles each of you will play in the company and the compensation each of you will earn once money comes. A founding team who builds their business on trust is building on a solid foundation.

Starting a business is a subject for an entirely different book, and there are plenty of great resources out there. Whether you're ready to create your own business or not, you have the power to pick the right road and drive all of your efforts in a focused direction forward. Choosing a North Star makes this job search completely different from any of your previous experiences. Once you name your new North Star, it's time to tell every person you can reach who you are. It's time to market yourself.

CHAPTER 5

Marketing Yourself

One CEO who hired my firm to lead an executive search sent a wish list of preferred attributes—in addition to all the requirements our candidates needed to match for the job. Her inspired list speaks volumes about why a boring cover letter and typical résumé are never going to be enough to get a decision maker excited about moving you to the front of the line for a job interview. This leader wanted us to present people who were smart, humble, secure, thoughtful, creative, kind, driven, and funny. This tall order makes you want to be around this type of candidate, imagining how magnetic they'd be.

Everybody has their prime strengths as a professional. The marketing strategies in this chapter zero in on your superpowers to make sure every potential boss can see them clearly. So many job seekers share a similar concern: "I'm not good at selling myself." This is a challenge I can help you face, and it's a skill you need to master.

One of the reasons many of us cite a lack of selling skills is because we've never needed to use them.

Friends and former colleagues often made the essential connections that led to our new jobs. But I'm guessing you bought this book because that method didn't work this time. Most of us never had formal training to learn how to brand our professional skills. Even if you've taken a course, or read a book on the subject, you're likely out of practice, or not up-to-date with newer strategies that work better now. Economic downturns and heavy periods of high unemployment increase the competition for every job. Your selling skills need to be hardwired directly into your new North Star. You have to make it repeatedly clear to everyone who considers you to be a legitimate job candidate that you have the qualifications, achievements, and focus they seek.

Let's deconstruct doubts about marketing yourself. If you're looking for a new job without enough prospects or leads to create the right opportunities, why do you feel uncomfortable about putting yourself out there? Effective, positive, self-promotion in the digital and physical world help you position and sell the skills you have to offer. People can't hire you if they don't see you. The most effective selling and marketing strategies raise you up above every candidate who's sitting home staring at their phone waiting for miracles. This crash course to promote your professional rebrand includes:

- A new résumé

- The strongest LinkedIn profile

- The perfect headshot

- The right wardrobe

- A new bio

- Convincing recommendations

- A killer cover letter

When you lose your job, your ego takes a serious hit. You need to tap more inner strength and willpower, restoring maximum confidence to succeed. The ego gets a bad rap when used to describe someone who is way too full of themselves. Yours can be a force for good. Let it shine. There's a line between self-promotion and self-aggrandizement. When you market yourself in the right way, you will *not* turn into a self-involved monster. If you don't become your own best champion, you're missing the chance to be seen as the next hot draft pick.

The most successful people you admire all learned to balance their *actual* work with the equally essential task of talking about what they're doing and accomplishing. That means doing all the necessary marketing, promotion, and publicity to make you aware of their contributions in the first place. This is true for every company leader, for entrepreneurs, politicians, Hollywood stars—but it's not just required of them anymore, it's for all of us. Marketing is your second, but equally important job. I once interviewed Danny DeVito for a television series I was producing at the time. He shared an insight that the studios pay top talent "the big money" not just because they need star power to sell the shows. Danny said that executives knew most actors would secretly work for free, just because they loved the magic. The big bucks came with big commitments from every actor to promote the living hell out of their projects on nonstop interviews and press tours. Embrace the idea that marketing yourself is not something reserved for movie stars and oversized egos. Effective self-promotion is the only way to unlock more job leads, interviews, and offers.

In chapter 4, you did the essential work to find your North Star. Now you're going to learn how to reach your chosen destination by reshaping the way you tell your professional story. Based on your North Star, you'll decide what to emphasize and what to omit on your LinkedIn and résumé.

As a headhunter, I've met some of the most accomplished pros who bring great work histories to the table— along with some of the most poorly written résumés and LinkedIn profiles. The reason most candidates' marketing materials aren't working well is because people get brainwashed into using the same tired language everyone else does. LinkedIn experts and résumé writing pros all subscribe to the belief that you have to have the maximum number of hot keywords in order to be found by every relevant search engine, robot, or junior human resources manager. While their faith in this "wide net" mentality won't harm you, their rewrites of your history leave every résumé and LinkedIn looking like a stale imitation of all the rest in the world's largest pile of sameness. Nothing could be more wrongheaded when it comes to the competitive environment of landing a good job. Your most important marketing tools need originality, inventiveness, personality, surprise, and even (if it suits) delight. You can use the right keywords to win the search engine sweepstakes, but most importantly, you can learn to stand out with your own unique personality that gets you to the front of the line.

This approach gets you noticed by the people who make the actual hiring decisions. I want you to sound like your *true* self, like you're talking directly to the boss on the page—not like you're stuck in some kind of antique, black-and-white movie with clichéd dialogue:

> "I have a very strong work ethic, and believe that my excellent oral and written communication skills can truly be an asset to your company." Get ready to throw all this tired résumé-speak into the digital trash bin. Please delete everything sounding like this: "A seasoned executive, with over eighteen years of experience and a proven track record with a demonstrated history of success at boring you to death. I take every project from inception to completion. I'm always on budget and on time and I am award-winning!"

Imagine how hiring managers react to the use of stale, boring résumé language. That's right, like zombies! If your résumé and LinkedIn profile don't produce an immediate positive response to convince the hiring manager you could be right for the job, there's no second chance. Don't say you have "excellent oral and writing skills." Show those skills by presenting excellent content to read. Don't say you have a "proven track record of success." Show the real details and stats that make your track record a slam-dunk argument.

The Clock Is Ticking

When I worked at MTV back in the day, we were accused of fueling a short attention span culture with our non-stop, fast-cutting sound and vision. Guilty as charged. By now, the world has gotten used to consuming media on every screen at the fastest possible speeds. We demand instant gratification and multiple choices to access all the information available to read, watch, or listen to. This frenetic pace has penetrated the fabric of our lives.

If you've ever been brave enough to swim in the deep waters of dating sites, you've suffered the "swipe left" culture. The next potential romantic partner of your dreams can choose to connect with you, or not, in exactly *one second*. When it comes to the job hunt, if you're lucky, you get somewhere between one and thirty seconds to be judged by anyone on LinkedIn. Are you ready to not screw this up? I'll show you how.

Tighten Your History

Before I jump into specifics let me address the number one question I am asked when helping clients rework their LinkedIn profiles and résumés: Do I need to list every job?

No. Anyone who tells you anything different is simply wrong.

If your résumé and LinkedIn profile don't produce an immediate positive response to convince the hiring manager you could be right for the job, there's no second chance.

Many of my fellow professional résumé writers and LinkedIn experts advise clients with long work histories not to go further back than about ten to twelve years. They presume that by eliminating all of the earliest positions they'd sidestep all those closet ageists—hiring managers who refuse to consider candidates who may be "overqualified," "too experienced," "too expensive," or, in their view, "too old" for the job.

If you have work history that travels back more than fifteen years, just drop the oldest jobs in your career and remove the years from the education section.

Also, do not list early jobs that are far off course from your current North Star. For example, if your career goal is currently focused on public relations, consistent with your most recent roles, but your earliest jobs after college were in the landscaping business, there's no benefit to listing the landscaping gigs. You're not going to be losing out by deleting any work history that's irrelevant. Instead, you're going to keep hiring managers' eyes on the ball.

What About Gaps of Employment?

Most job-seeking candidates are extremely concerned about showing any unemployment gaps on their résumés and LinkedIn profiles. Gaps in your job history naturally open up during any prolonged period of unemployment. Whether you were terminated for any reason, or you left on your own, these gaps can cause considerable stress.

The tightest presentation of your work history will remove opportunities for the reader to stop and wonder what went wrong. You don't want the hiring manager to ask too many questions about the transitions from one job to the next. Every time you have to answer complicated questions about how you got each job and why you left, you waste extremely valuable time in your thirty-minute interview. Making all of this essential information clear on the page removes the uncertainty and keeps everything moving faster during the interview.

Gaps in your work experience may be due to parental or medical leave, personal time off, world travel, alien abduction . . . the list goes on. But the more you find ways to answer these questions right on the page of your résumé, in a seamless rewrite, the more time you'll save to get the interviewers talking with you about their company and the role you want to fill now. (See chapter 9 for your master class on nailing the perfect, thirty-minute job interview).

Hanging a Shingle

One of the most effective strategies for filling gaps in your work history is to "hang a shingle." You never want to leave too long a stretch of time remaining blank in your story. Even if you've never incorporated as an independent business officially, you can declare yourself an independent business person on your LinkedIn and your résumé. Prove that you are not afraid to demonstrate the entrepreneurial 'tude we highlighted in chapter 4. Hanging a shingle is as simple as naming an entity under which you want to present that you are conducting business. Your company name can be as obvious as Rob Barnett Media. Or you can be as creative as you like in choosing a name that fits your own firm. There are a number of easy, inexpensive ways to establish an independent company with formal documentation and standing with your state and federal tax identifications. But there's nobody stopping you from branding and positioning yourself within an hour of reading this chapter without any formal documentation.

Choose a company name. Get a friend to design a logo. Create a company page on LinkedIn describing what kind of business you do, and of course give yourself the title that best represents the work that you've decided you want to do in your newly defined North Star.

For example, if your most recent positions were as a head chef in restaurants, but you've only been able to work private events for the past two years, brand your own business and take credit for any work you've done independently by naming your current "company" and title at the top of your résumé and LinkedIn profile. This way you'll be identified as Jane Doe, owner and operator of Meals by Jane, and no one will judge the two-year gap in your employment history.

One of our clients, Kari, was hired as an account director at an advertising tech firm. After a sudden change at her company, hundreds of employees were sent packing—including Kari.

Days after losing her job, Kari, a Brooklyn newly-
wed, learned she was pregnant. She first reached out to
me a few months after her baby girl was born. She had
taken a part-time position at an online, nonprofit art
school. We had an initial strategy session about Kari's
career path forward, the search for her North Star, and
a full-time job. We revised her job history and rebuilt
her professional brand.

Kari had an inspiring, positive personality. She was
magnetic. One of my jobs was to get that energy onto the
digital page—and replace the tired old résumé-speak
with the sound of the real person behind it.

Kari worked with me to rewrite her material with
flair and personality. We created a new version of her
LinkedIn and résumé, which was dramatically better than the typical boredom you normally see. We
included phrases like, "Most of my career has been
blueprint-free"—to show that Kari was always reinvent-
ing. We included stats that recruiters like on résumés:
"Overnight audience growth . . . of seventy percent." We
polished her LinkedIn off with a fun finish: "I'm still
working on recording my name more confidently at
the beginning of conference calls. But let's get in touch
anyway."

Once we revamped Kari's job history, it was time to
determine her North Star. She held previous roles with
the simple title, social media manager, but I wanted Kari
to capture a more senior role, based on her best skills
and past success. I advised her to hang her own shingle

and send the strong message that she was running her own growth marketing firm. This way, her part-time job could legitimately be presented as a client for Kari's business, and her résumé no longer had to show a job gap. By hanging a shingle and presenting her own firm, Kari could now be considered for a wider range of work.

One of the hardest issues we all face when we're out of work is that we lose leverage to negotiate. We lose some desirability too. When people know you're out of work and available for . . . anything, a hiring manager can offer you less than you're worth.

When you claim your own North Star, you regain that leverage to be better positioned for what's next. Kari hung her shingle. Exactly eight weeks later, to the day, I got this email:

> Hey Rob, Just a thank-you for nudging me to go all in on my LinkedIn as an agency founder. This quickly led to a paid social team training with another PR agency. Now . . . a six-figure, five-month project for me to run as "my agency." Exciting times. Big thanks. Kari

You can fill significant gaps anywhere on your LinkedIn and résumé. Just remember to obey the rules my mom and dad would want you to follow. Don't lie. Don't create independent jobs and work projects that never existed. However, make sure to include every and any projects you pursued on your own during gaps of official employment, giving the details of work that you may have developed and produced for others during any stage in between jobs.

Mastering LinkedIn

If you're not getting the responses and interviews you need from the most important real estate in the world of job search, your LinkedIn is ready for a digital makeover. Until someone invents a better product to knock LinkedIn off of its pedestal, this platform is the first place most hiring managers go to assess who you are as a professional, and whether or not you could be a part of their team.

Your LinkedIn profile is even more important than your résumé because it's the first, fastest, and easiest way for anybody to form an opinion about who you are. If you're successful at making this first impression, you'll have the chance to get to the next logical steps in the hiring process, which include submitting a résumé and cover letter. You've got to win here first. If getting your next, best job is a poker game, then your table stakes to play start by ponying up the most compelling LinkedIn profile.

Don't be scared. We may not throw your current LinkedIn baby out with the bathwater. But you're not about to experience a long, luxurious, candlelit bubble bath. We have heavy scrubbing to do on your profile photo, your graphics, your About section, and the entire work journey listed in the Experience section. Every job you've ever had needs to be reevaluated and reframed, with a radical focus on knowing what to leave in, what to delete, and how to add the content needed to (1) make the immediate best impression and (2) get the right responses. Everything you present on LinkedIn needs to support the decision you've made in chapter 4 on your new North Star.

Your next, best job will be listed in the headline of LinkedIn right under your profile photo and your name. From top to bottom, you're about to learn how to best present your education, skills, and interests. And we're going to bring it all home by teaching you how to get glowing recommendations that convince the right minds you've already done the work they need from you now.

Remember that in both your LinkedIn and your résumé, you alone are in total control of what details of your past employment you want to share with the world.

Whenever I work with clients to rewrite a professional background, I let them know that I've got both of my parents looking down on me from the great beyond. My mom was a schoolteacher, and while I was growing up, she'd refuse to read any homework I submitted if there was even one instance of a minor typo, bad grammar, or faulty punctuation. Most importantly, my mom watches over every résumé and LinkedIn I write for people with her ultimate cardinal rule: Never, ever lie. Then there's my dad. The other guy watching me from up above while I drive the rewrites of clients' professional careers was one of the well-known "Mad Men" of Madison Avenue's golden age. My dad was a professional master of spinning a marketing message in the most effective way to move an audience to want to buy anything that was being sold. Dad wants you to look away from this book for a minute and see everything you bought that makes you feel good. You knew these things existed and you made a decision to purchase everything you own because of successful marketing. Dad needs you to start selling yourself.

The Big Secret

Approximately 98 percent of the clients who hire my firm to reinvent their LinkedIn profiles have no clue that the largest amount of space available for customized visual branding is sitting right up at the top of their page. Look for the extra-large rectangle sitting right behind your profile photo. For some reason, almost every person I've ever met has no idea that this generic background provides the same customizable functionality as the cover photo everyone *does* seem to know how to use on Facebook.

The few people using this large area for eye-catching mojo are going to be noticed exponentially more than everyone using the generic LinkedIn background. But, don't make the mistake of going all in on a photo by mother nature (unless you're employed to save the environment).

Your background photo should be a visual complement to the North Star you've chosen in chapter 4. For example, if you've decided that your career path is Yoga instructor, then your LinkedIn cover photo would be the best shot of you teaching a class with students. If your North Star is finance director, then you should not use an image of Wrigley Field just because you live in the great city of Chicago. I love the Cubs, but in order to have the best representation of your professional brand, consider creating a simple background with the logos of the most prominent companies where you've worked in finance to bring your career credibility to life.

One last tip about this cover photo: LinkedIn has a tendency to size images differently on the mobile app than on desktop. Make sure the cover photo you choose is sized correctly for desktop and phone. It's easy to adjust the photos so that you're not covering up the most important part of the image you selected, and you don't want your profile photo (headshot) fighting with this cover photo for space.

Your Profile Photo

Here's an essential checklist to make sure you're using a photo most capable of having the work world fall in love with your beautiful face:

- **Quality:** You don't need to hire a professional photographer and spend any money on your headshot as long as you do not use any photographs that are the least bit blurry, especially if the viewer zooms in to expand the photo. Anything shot on an iPhone 8 series or better will do fine. If you decide to go pro, seek out friends who are professional photographers willing to give you the best deal on a simple headshot session.

- **Expression:** Your eyes should be directly facing the person looking at your photograph. Smile. I mean, smile as if you're looking at someone you really like and admire. Let's see those pearly whites. Please look straight into the camera. No supermodel glances off to the side or anything wacky, unless you're a comic, an actor, or a supermodel.

- **Indoor Background:** No outdoor photos for the headshot. No vacation shots. Use an image taken inside with a nondescript background that won't detract in any way from your beautiful face.

- **Cropping:** Now that you've gone to the trouble of picking the perfect background, make sure to use only the tiniest bit of that background when you crop and post the final image on LinkedIn. You barely want to see anything above and around your full headshot and you don't want to go any farther down than just showing a little bit below your neck. It's a headshot, not a body shot.

- **Clothing:** The right version of business casual is best. Not too business. Not too casual.

The About Section—Your New Bio

You have a priceless opportunity to bring your entire story together in what LinkedIn calls the *About* section. I suggest three short paragraphs that give any potential hiring manager the most important information about who you are, where you've been, and what you've accomplished. Three perfect paragraphs can communicate all you need to make the most impact and market yourself. Since the About section is so close to the top of your LinkedIn profile, this section is going to be read most often, especially by the busiest people who may not have time to scroll all the way down to study every job you list in the Experience section. My strongest suggestion is to write your About story using a first-person, active voice. Treat this precious real estate as if you are talking directly to the person who's going to hire you. Put yourself in the mind of an actual face-to-face pitch. And I'm begging you, please drop the instinct to write like the robot everyone else chooses to be.

Your About section doubles as your new bio. Since this precedes the experience section on your LinkedIn profile, you are free from the chronology of the full work history down below. The About section is non-linear. It doesn't matter *when* you achieved one of the most impressive victories in your career. It matters most that you spotlight the best you have to offer, no matter how recent or early you had success.

Paragraph 1—Your Superpowers

Here's where you make the first impression and the best understanding of your strongest professional attributes and skills. Most people I work with have a very hard time bragging about themselves (in general, but also) in this first paragraph. A little coaxing usually reveals superpowers. I start by asking clients to imagine that I've just given their previous managers and coworkers a heavy dose of truth serum and laughing gas. I've also hypnotized them and they are in my total control. They're instructed to brag on your behalf about all the things that made you an excellent contributor to the company. Once you can imagine that scenario, ideas begin to flow about the strongest compliments you've been paid on the job, and you can start a first draft of paragraph 1. Keep the sentences succinct, punchy, and jargon free. Be confident, but not boastful.

If your North Star is chief marketing officer, your first paragraph might read:

> I'm a strategic marketing leader dedicated to clear and consistent messaging rooted in first-class consumer insights. Brands only win their rightful share of voice and revenue if every employee is communicating internally and externally with the same clarity and passion for the mission. My teams know I'm a leader they can trust to share all the details needed to meet the objective. Every coworker knows that I'm tough, fair, driven, and unafraid to share the credit.

My experience as an entrepreneur has taught me to maximize every available resource to succeed.

Paragraph 2—Your Journey

Here's your most important work history, presented in a tight summary of your past jobs. Use the same first-person voice and speak in real sentences. There's no need to include all your jobs here, just the ones that stand out most. And you definitely don't need to include your oldest, junior jobs in this About section. If you do choose to include one or more early gigs after college, just a brief sentence will do, as long as these previous positions still support your new North Star narrative. Here's an example of a succinct paragraph 2:

> I started my career as a marketing manager for *Parents* magazine. I was then hired by *Vogue* as an integrated marketing director. My eight years included multiple digital launches, and I developed and led *Vogue*'s very first app. I was senior director of brand marketing for Loft by Ann Taylor, overseeing brand strategy, insights, editorial, and all social media marketing. I was then promoted to head of marketing for all Ann Taylor brands in 2014.

Think of your second About paragraph as a short, "just the facts" journey. Cut out anything extraneous that might slow it down or confuse the reader with unnecessary tangents or less relevant details. For some of you, synthesizing a life's work may feel challenging. I encourage you to be brutal and stick to the highpoints only. Think less about all you want the world to know and more about giving a busy, dispassionate hiring manager the essentials.

One more tip: If your last job was the most impressive position in your journey, you may want to start paragraph 2 in the present and work backward. Or, first job to the last job also works fine.

Paragraph 3—Your Greatest Hits

Picture this finishing touch like the "Pearly Gates" swinging open to lead you into your next, best job. Here are your "greatest hits." Write a few sentences about the one or two most significant accomplishments of your career—showcasing your proudest victories from a few of your previous positions with the most current relevance to your new North Star and the expertise companies need most from you now. Examples:

- I was awarded Condé Nast Marketer of the Year for the creation of *Vogue TV*, the brand's first digital video content platform.

- My team delivered the consumer insights, new product strategy, positioning, and branding for Loft, contributing to 75 percent annual sales growth.

- I led all marketing for the first *Teen Vogue* Summit, a one-of-a-kind experience dedicated to activism, innovation, and creation. Speakers,

including Hillary Rodham Clinton, presented
programs on grassroots organizing, STEM
careers, and civic leadership.

No matter how long your career has been until now, the best formula for your About section is to pack the most powerful punches you've got into these three short paragraphs. Tell them about your superpowers, share your best jobs on the journey, and sing your top two or three greatest hits. That's it.

It's important to keep this as tight as you can. Brevity is your best friend on LinkedIn. There's no time to lose stating anything typical and obvious. We know you're a professional. We know you're experienced. And for God's sake, we know you're "looking for your next opportunity." Please don't waste time stating any of these ideas as a badge of honor.

Paragraph 4—Skills (optional)

Although LinkedIn provides a section called Skills, it tends to be buried lower down the page. For search purposes, it's fine to list any legitimate, applicable skills. If you want to add an optional fourth section to your About, please don't add every obvious skill like "Microsoft Word." The skills you highlight as keywords should reinforce superpowers you showed in paragraph 1. You can simply create a fourth paragraph as a list. Examples:

Brand design

Event marketing

Social media strategy

Consumer insights

Audience development

Once you've completed your new About section, you're ready to start rewriting your work history in the Experience section. A quick note before we begin. Don't worry that you've already used some of the most impressive information about your career in the About section. You're going to use it again. As above, so below.

Experience Section

Your current and previous work history is listed in the Experience section starting with the most recent position at the top and your earliest jobs down below. You've got seven places to add information:

- Company Logo
- Job Title
- Company Name
- Dates of Employment
- Location
- Description
- Media

Let's take a look at each.

➤ **Company Logo:** As long as the place of business where you worked has their own LinkedIn company page, that logo will populate once you enter the company's name on your own LinkedIn profile. If the place of business does not have their own page, then LinkedIn will simply fill the logo area with a generic image.

➤ **Job Title:** List the exact job title you were officially given by the company.

➤ **Company Name:** This is simple and straightforward; however, when you start to enter the company name, as we said above, the logo should populate and you'll want to select the correct choice that you're given.

➤ **Dates of Employment:** You can simplify your LinkedIn and résumé for the rest of your working life by giving up the old, conventional approach of listing the exact start and end dates of every previous job, including the month, date, and year. I recommend only using the years in this field of information. Benefits become apparent if you had brief tenures of employment. For example: If you started a position in June 2019 that ended abruptly in January 2020, LinkedIn shows the world that job only lasted seven months. By simply listing the start date as 2019 and the end date as 2020, you avoid waving the biggest red flag prompting every interviewer to ask, "What happened there?" You'll still be asked why the job only covers 2019–2020, but it won't scream seven months. And you're not lying on the page. Similarly, if you started a job in October 2016 and left in January 2020, LinkedIn shows you were in the position three years and three months. If you only list the years 2016 to 2020, four years are noted by LinkedIn. These are facts, not lies. And my job is to make sure you're doing everything you can do to make the best impression. Interviewers rarely ask exactly what month each job began. If so, you'll answer truthfully as best as you remember.

➤ **Location:** List the location of the company where you worked. If you worked remotely, then you can list the location for the main headquarters of the business and mention more detail in your description section.

➤ **Description:** The rubber meets the road right here. You start earning more job interviews once you improve your writing about every previous position listed in the Experience section. The best way to present a clear, quick snapshot of each job you've held in the past is to break the information into two distinct parts. The first part should stay focused on the primary responsibilities and the core function of the role. For example, if you listed "National Insurance Broker," an opening, very short paragraph of a sentence or two could read: *I provide customized insurance solutions to meet*

*your goals to protect the health and legacy for you
and your family.* After the initial description of what
you do, add an extra space for easy readability
and then include a bulleted list of specific
achievements and accomplishments during your
time in this job.

The number of individual highlights you add should be
in proportion to the amount of time you spent on this
particular job. For example, if you worked as a national
insurance broker for this one firm for approximately six
years, you need to claim at least three major achievements. If you held this one position for more than ten
years, I would not recommend adding more than five
or six bullet points calling out your best success. Every
section of your LinkedIn and résumé need to be as concise as possible.

The achievements and accomplishments you add
under every job in your Experience section must be
the most impressive, specific highlights. Far too many
people believe that being a "liaison" with "interde-
partmental skills" who has "attended meetings with
senior managers" and "written reports" about work is
worthy proof of success. Please take this with all the
love intended: If you promote basic skills as evidence
of expertise you're falling short. Any bullet point you
list in your work experience has to be a true milestone
of success. For example, our insurance broker bullets
could be:

- Elected president of the West Coast Regional Healthcare Research Association.

- Increased annual revenue in 2020 by 25 percent.

- Launched new long-term disability offering thirty days before deadline.

The achievements and accomplishments listed in bullet points in the description of each job of your work experience should name names, business partnerships, specific increases in customers acquired or revenues generated. Support every success point with as much factual evidence as you can.

➤ **Media:** LinkedIn provides users the ability to upload video, articles, photos, presentations, audio, and any other media that allow hiring managers to see the fruits of your labors come to life beyond just the black-and-white words on the digital page. Please make the best use of this opportunity to bring any of your most impressive projects to life for the people who are considering hiring you to deliver on their behalf. Video is best if you have any short clips that feature you speaking in any professional setting. If you've ever been featured prominently in articles about your work, this is the perfect place to showcase your best press by uploading a few examples right onto your LinkedIn profile.

Education Section

Unless you're a recent graduate, remove the years that you went to college. Keep all the most interesting information about degrees and affiliations that matter, but drop the years you attended. The ageists can't judge you. And if it has been as long as fifteen or twenty years since college, you don't need to list all of the ancient jobs you took right after graduation in the Experience section— especially if they don't support your new North Star.

Recommendations

Don't overlook one of the best ways to sing your praises: having other professionals sing on your behalf. LinkedIn recommendations are easy to give and get. I always joke with clients that it's a lot easier to ask a colleague for a righteous shoutout than it is to borrow money. Think about people you've worked for, and those who have worked for you and with you throughout your career. The beauty of the way LinkedIn works is that the most recent recommendations you've been given will populate at the top of the list. So even if you worked for a great boss many years ago, they can tell the world about your value as a professional now. A recommendation written now will carry the date it was posted and not the date when you worked with the person giving the recommendation. If people you knew back in the day have impressive and prominent positions now, their recommendations about your character will have a positive impact on any potential hiring manager considering you as a candidate. Be a giver and not just a taker. If you

129

ask friends and coworkers to give you a rock-solid recommendation on LinkedIn, please do the same for them.

Résumé Rules

Your LinkedIn profile is the first place most professionals look to decide if you've got something they need. Immediate online access to your job history by any future boss may make you think you no longer need a formal résumé. Despite every technical advancement available in a job search, a great résumé is still the gold standard all hiring managers request to assess your candidacy and circulate the document to others within the company. Before we get started on the overhaul to make your résumé rock, let me sing you a sad song I've heard too many times before.

The Bad Résumé Blues

Please, Dear Hiring Manager, lend me your ears.
I'm thrilled to apply with experience of over fifteen years.

My proven track record will show you success.
My dedication and passion is impossible to suppress.

Oral and written communication skills are a plus.
Just wait till you hear about my demonstrated history of trust.

If these buzzwords sound like you've heard it before,
you're probably right. I'm an absolute bore.

Thanks for your time.
I hope to hear soon.
My landlord says I'm evicted in June.

I don't want this to be your soundtrack, so let's have at it.

First, let's settle the great controversy about a one-page résumé. One page is fine. Two pages are just as fine. Don't buy into the popular idea that you've got to have a one-pager. If your career history is brief, it makes perfect sense. But if you've been working for many years at more than four or five companies, it's going to be almost impossible to squeeze all of your important information onto a single page. Worry more about readability, normal spacing, and decent font sizes looking great on a two-page résumé. Don't go with a bad, overcrowded look just to stay on one page. But please, there's no justification for a three-pager, or anything longer. You'll be freaking the reader out with anything more than a few pages. Second, if you have to choose between substance and style, the look of your résumé should always take a backseat to the quality of the content. Don't spend too much time obsessing over how to format and design a successful résumé. There's no magic bullet here. And if you spend days deciding fonts, point size, margins, and graphics, you're going to end up losing your mind. Look for simple, easy-to-read examples online that appeal to your sensibility. If your instinct is to go for a more flashy style, you may want to hire someone to do this for you. The investment will save you time if you don't have the skills on your own to do this kind of work. But there are many free options you can find online that will get the job done.

Strap on your seat belt. Here are my best résumé rules.

Your Name

Yes, I feel a little silly needing to talk about your name, but I do have a very strong point of view about this topic. I was reworking a résumé and a LinkedIn profile for a man named Stuart Miller. I asked him if I could call him Stu. Then I asked if anyone called him Stuart except his mom. They did not. Then I asked if everyone in the workplace called him Stu. They did. Stuart's name on his résumé, his LinkedIn profile—and everywhere else on paper, online, or on social media—should be: Stu Miller. Don't match your résumé and all of your digital real estate and marketing materials with your driver's license or your birth certificate. These are the first rules of professional branding and marketing. Be consistent. Be personable. Do not be legally formal when you're building and promoting your personal and professional brand. If you alternate maiden names and married names in your personal and professional lives, then make sure you're consistent in your professional life. Your job getting hired now is infinitely harder if people have a hard time knowing who you are and how to find you online in any way they want, without a second of confusion.

Headline

I've almost never seen a résumé that didn't start with everyone's contact info at the very top of the page. I rarely see a résumé with the second most important piece of information—second only to your name—front and center. In chapter 4, you found your North Star.

Now you need to have your new professional headline clear and bold on any version of your résumé. For that matter, everywhere you look, people should see your North Star. For example, at the top of my résumé is: Rob Barnett, Headhunter.

Contact Information

There's a new normal I've been seeing and liking. In an online age, where it often feels like we've lost most of our privacy, there's no longer a need to put your entire street address on your résumé. You should definitely include your best personal or professional email address. Always list your cell number. I highly recommend adding the URL that clicks through to your LinkedIn profile. And finally, city and state. If you are applying to a position in another country, add your current country of residence. Besides LinkedIn, I don't recommend adding any other social media links to your résumé. In all you do, less is more.

Summary or Profile

I encourage all of our clients to include a brief paragraph at the top of the résumé before the experience section begins. Some prefer to use the word *Summary*. I prefer Profile. A summary that duplicates too much of the job information you'll see in the résumé is redundant and takes up valuable space. A profile of your strongest superpowers, character traits, and one to three greatest achievements is the most prominent opportunity to make the best impression. Go back and look at the information we discussed in the

About section of LinkedIn. Adapt what you wrote in paragraph 1 and remove the first-person voice to nail your best profile on top of the résumé.

Experience

I'm about to drop a simplicity bomb of love on your head. Ready? All you need to do is copy and paste your entire Experience section from the LinkedIn profile directly onto your résumé. Who do you love? This guy. There's no need for any difference on the two documents.

Education

Love me again. Copy and paste the same information from LinkedIn onto the résumé.

That's it!

Cover Letters

Welcome to this century. I don't know why most cover letters sound like they were written ages ago. I'm always in favor of professionalism, but I never want to see all your hopes and dreams die on the digital page if you send anything as stilted as this:

> To Whom It May Concern,
>
> I am thrilled to be applying for the position of Regional Sales Manager with your firm. I have fourteen years of experience in your industry and a demonstrated history of success.

I am a dependable, hardworking team leader committed to delivering excellent results in everything I do. I was recently laid off by my last firm after a downsizing. I would like to request an interview at your earliest convenience. My résumé is attached for your review. I look forward to hearing from you soon.

Sincerely,

[Person Who Does Not Win This Year's Cover Letter of the Year Award]

If you're still writing anything remotely close to the specimen above, don't worry—we'll fix it.

———

Let's start with the person you're addressing the letter to. Don't bother sending covers to "Dear Hiring Manager" or "Whom It May Concern." You're losing any momentum and inspiration before you've even started. Take the time to find out exactly who the hiring manager is for the role you're applying for before you consider writing a cover letter to Mrs. or Mr. Generic. LinkedIn, Google, and the company website(s) are the obvious first places to start putting on your detective gear and finding out who's making the decision in the places where you want to apply. I'd also prefer you wait to write your cover letter until after you've successfully had at least one or more contacts with another employee at the company who knows the boss, or any mutual connections you can find. A warm, connected cover letter will beat a cold first approach every time for two reasons. The hiring manager will be much more open to connecting with someone who has been referred by a person they respect. And every time you can get more direct information about the company you're pitching from another employee in advance of the cover letter you have 1,000 percent better odds. You'll be able to speak with knowledge about what's most important to them. You'll replace all the typical blah blah with proof that you know what's going on in that business. The biggest mistake in cover letters is writing like a robot instead of communicating exactly as if you were speaking directly to the person you may be working for. Another mistake is to write primarily about yourself without devoting as much content, if not *more,* to proving you know the business, their needs, and where you can bring value.

Please don't turn your cover letter into another version of your résumé by filling it with all of what you've done in the past. There's room to put some context into why your experience is right for the position without telling your life story. But the cover letter is always a companion to your résumé, not a carbon copy.

Ideally, a cover letter should fit on one page. In most cases, too long a letter scares hiring executives away. There are some instances where turning the cover letter into a deeper pitch, with ideas and proposals for what you'd do if you were in the position, is advised. But most businesses expect to see a brief, one-page cover.

Before I give you an example of a cover letter to use as a guide, I'm going to recommend a point of style that may or may not meet with your tastes. After more than five decades working for companies big and small, I'm never looking for anyone to call me Mr. Barnett in any correspondence. It's just too formal. "Dear Rob" or "Hi Rob" beats anything else. I believe you'll have more success with less formality and the first-name method. It's your call.

Here's a cover letter I would want to receive from someone applying to my company. I hope you find ideas you can adapt or improve upon:

Dear Rob,

I just finished reading *Next Job, Best Job* and wanted to reach out to thank you for the ideas and inspiration to focus my career path. Your book made me realize that I've spent the last few years sending out two or three different versions of my résumé for roles that were lined up with some of my previous work experience, but not clearly focused enough on a North Star to win these positions.

I'm applying to be your new Head of Social Media. I was surprised to learn that your current team at Rob Barnett Media did not have a person leading this effort. And I can only guess that you're spending a ton of your own time managing this essential aspect of your communication strategy on your own. I did see that you have a great marketing and publicity firm supporting the promotion of your book.

I've most recently served as the head of social media for [Company A]. Like you, our business is dedicated to helping place full-time employees in executive and staff positions. We also provide some of the services for job candidates that you currently offer on your website. My earlier positions in social media included great runs with [Company B] and [Company C]. I've attached a résumé for review and I'd love to ask you for a twenty-minute-intro call in the weeks ahead to explore whether we could be a good fit.

Thanks again for *Next Job, Best Job.*

> Talk soon,
> [Person Who Just Wrote a
> Great Cover Letter]

Here's how the three paragraphs above can help you write better cover letters:

1. This person started off about the company.
    They took the time to know what this book was about and explained how its core premise was embraced. This reveal came with a nice touch of humility and ended with a strong segue to their availability and interest.

2. A direct pitch for the job with evidence of more homework and a sincere offer of service.

3. Add recent and most relevant experience.
    Refer to the résumé for more. Add final touches:

Request a brief, twenty-minute call (patiently) in the weeks ahead (without desperation) and an easy ask to explore if it's a good fit.

Clarity, Confidence, Commitment

One last tip: Most cover letters are too shy and lack enough *confidence*. Add a few more C's to the mix: *clarity* and *commitment*. Be confident that you're right for the job. Reread the draft over and over. Revise. Improve it. Perfect it. Have friends you trust proofread for total clarity. Show commitment. Communicate that you're ready, willing, and able to make a full commitment.

Do I need to say that one typo equals death? There, I said it.

A Tribe Called *Next*

Every independent hero in our culture needs a tribe. If your current job search feels like you're stuck in quicksand, our next chapter will reach down with two strong hands to pull you out. The day I decided to share my shame, fear, anger, and hurt online with anyone willing to listen was the day my life changed. The response to my first video fueled a constant flow of energy from people all needing a new way to find the right work—together.

Our next chapter will show you how to gather a tribe to suit up for battle and win the work we all deserve. When you join people who've made the leap from loneliness into a network of superpros, you'll realize that you are not stuck in this fight alone.

CHAPTER 6

Find Your Tribe

In *Star Trek: The Wrath of Khan,* Spock says, "Logic clearly dictates that the needs of the many outweigh the needs of the few." Captain Kirk answers, "Or the one."

When I posted my very first spontaneous video about being out of work, I realized that my need to find the next, best job was the same struggle too many friends were going through at that moment. I gazed up at the *Star Trek* poster from the original TV series that's been hanging on my wall since I was twelve years old. Trek philosophy about "the needs of the many" rang in my ear. It made me realize I should be reaching out beyond my own needs. That first video got a ton more views than I'd expected, and I kept posting new episodes every day. The following built a tribe of job seekers that changed my career and my life.

Your job search does not have to be a solo, isolating experience. Who made the crappy rule that you have to hunker down alone or depressed in a job search without any significant human support? There's strength in numbers. When you reach out to other people, you find that almost everyone knows something about this issue. Each new contact can put another jigsaw piece into the puzzle to help you see what's next. The 2020 global pandemic gave us all a master class learning to use existing and new technology to stay connected, to build our networks, and to find our tribe.

I'm inviting you to join our tribe now. We call ourselves #iBJA (in between jobs, again). Let's get tribal.

If your instinct has been to only share the hardship of losing your job with a small circle of your closest friends, you're missing out on help from many people who've walked in your shoes before. Thousands of job loss experts in our tribe have learned how to make the quest for new work shorter and less painful. Good people you need by your side have earned battle scars during their own firing and hiring wars. And the best people are willing to help heal your wounds with the wisdom they've found to save you valuable time on your job search.

We discourage members of our tribe from wallowing in a pity party. Our like-minded pros are dedicated to working together on positive solutions to get people hired faster. When you pool your resources, you generate more job opportunities. By widening the circle of seekers, you all benefit. Joining or helping build a job search tribe is a powerful way to fight the funk. You'll be energized by trusted friends who hold members accountable for making progress—and making fun happen too. Job searching does not have to suck. Tap this collective soul power.

Our job search tribe has become a touchstone for me and everyone who decides to spend time inside. (I Googled "touchstone" and loved what I found: "determining the quality or genuineness of a thing / a fundamental or quintessential part / a test of authenticity or value of something intangible.") The support of more souls doing the same inner work to find the right answers helps replace what's not working in your current search and helps you get to what's next, faster.

The size of your tribe is not as important as the quality of the people in your circle. It only takes one magic human to change your future. You need active members who stay committed to finding the best ways to connect. Meaningful, regular communication provides the support and substantial job leads to speed your search.

Contacts from A to Z

I met another headhunter years ago who asked if I could remember the last time I had gone through every single contact in my phone. He suggested categorizing all of the contacts into an organized, trackable system during any job search. I'd never done this before. (The thought is daunting if you're more of a right brain person who recoils at the sight of a spreadsheet. If this idea for massive data organization fills you with dread, find someone with experience to help.)

The process of organizing every professional and personal connection in my main files, plus all of my LinkedIn connections, all Facebook "friends," followers on Instagram, Twitter, Vimeo, Venmo, PayPal, and on and on, was a task that seemed like it would take forever to complete. Why isn't there a button on a digital device that can do all this massive organization? I'm counting on one of you to hurry up and invent that, now, please?!

I can say with confidence, that it was worth every ounce of teeth grinding. As I went through all the lists, I was determined to reach out to every single person with a quick call, email, or text. It's good for the soul to reach out to friends and colleagues, and colleagues who become friends. And if you like to play the odds, scrolling through an organized contact list on a schedule will inevitably tip the numbers in your favor. Reaching out in a way that's true and real will bring the right people in to you. I don't know how many LinkedIn contacts you have, but when was the last time you went through them *all*, A to Z? My recommendation is to get through them all right away and figure out how to create real dialogue that can be useful for both of you. When this process starts to work and people start responding, you will quickly begin building your tribe. Others will begin to reach out to you for help. Please pay it forward by responding. Unless it's clearly spam, or a lame, random sales pitch that has nothing to do with your interest, a quick human reply will continue to widen your network and bring you one step closer to the goal of getting hired.

"The Art of Asking"

One of the hardest things for many of us to do is the simple act of asking for help. Some of us have a sense of shame when we lose our jobs, and others don't want to be a burden to people we care about who have their own problems. When you're hurting, it's easy to forget that there are people in your life right now who will stop everything they're doing and come when you call.

I learned about "the art of asking" from Amanda Palmer. She holds a heroic place in my heart as an inspiring musician, artist, author, and a force of constant connection for every one of us who follow her real-time adventures on social media (and at AmandaPalmer. net). In the early days of crowdfunding, Amanda raised a record-setting amount of money to finance an album through Kickstarter. Her TED talk about the power of asking for help earned millions of video views. Amanda shared her philosophy in the book, *The Art of Asking: How I Learned to Stop Worrying and Let People Help,* which debuted at number seven on the *New York Times* bestseller list. Her book has become one of my favorite go-to gifts for countless friends who need Amanda's inspired ideas about asking and giving.

I met Amanda through my friend Holly Cara Price who passed away during the writing of this book after an eleven-year heroic battle with cancer. One day in 2008, Holly called me and said that I had to drop everything and meet her in the city to go see an artist I'd never heard of before. When I hesitated, Holly said, "Rob. You know how you feel about Springsteen? I shouted back, "Holly, you can't say that to me. That's putting too much pressure on the show."

One of the hardest things for many of us to do is the simple act of asking for help.

But when I finally saw Amanda I wasn't disappointed. The lights went out in a small theater in the Chelsea section of New York City. The first notes of music we heard weren't coming from the stage. The sound was coming from behind us. We turned around to look, but the lights were all still out. Then a spotlight hit the singer up in the balcony dressed in ripped fishnets, strumming on a tiny ukulele. She wasn't singing through any microphone, but she was easily heard by all of us in the club. And as she sang, Amanda Palmer started climbing down the stairs from the balcony onto the back of the main floor of the hall where she walked slowly up through the entire crowd to take the stage. I was hooked.

Amanda welcomed the audience with a special thanks to the people who came earliest to the show to meet her in the ladies' room for "toilet confessionals." Can you imagine a better way to meet your favorite rock star? Privacy and intimacy in the unlikeliest of places for a spiritual confession. I wasn't privy to what went on during that bathroom meeting, but I could tell Amanda was unique.

When you follow Amanda Palmer on social media, you get a master class in the art of intimacy, transparency, and constant communication in the modern world. Amanda inspires everyone she reaches to get over the fear of asking people who care about you for the help you need. The ones who respond are the soulful warriors you need now. These are the new members of your tribe who'll call you when they need you most.

Losing your job is high up on the list of the most stressful events you face in your life. Don't travel this road alone. Find a tribe of people to help you get through the hardship and to support you on this journey. We all have a tendency to shy away from asking for help when we need it most. Trust me: Ask.

Tribal Video

The first tribal video I sent out to the world came in a short clip posted on LinkedIn and Facebook. I highly recommend brief, personal videos as the best method to communicate to build your own tribe of job-seeking super pros. If video is not your thing, there are other methods you can choose. I'm going to give you a series of options. But videos are seen by far more people online than posts that are only text-based, or even photos.

It's much easier than you think to create effective, personal videos on a regular basis. You want a high-quality image with a phone that isn't too outdated. Make sure you have decent lighting, clear sound, an engaging or nondescript background, and the ability to frame a relatively close image of your beautiful face.

Your videos will feel best for your viewers if you speak from the heart without a formal script. Think through what you want to say in advance, then say it. If you're new to the game, there's nothing wrong with rehearsing. Your video doesn't have to be Academy Award worthy; you just don't want it to completely suck. The key is to not obsessively overthink about making a short, personal video. A few flubs are going to score you more points for being human than recording a thousand versions of a short, heavily scripted message that you're trying to perform with ultimate perfection.

Let everyone know that you're building a new tribe of like-minded pros all looking for the next, best job. Ask people to send you an email if they want to join. Share a few simple rules for membership. The perfect starting price for admission is free. But you should let people know that membership comes with privileges and benefits including:

- Intros to the friends at companies they need to know

- Group support

- Tribal gatherings

- Free advice and more sounding boards

- Shared professional services (you do my taxes and I'll do your new website . . .)

Have fun with your videos. Be yourself and act natural. If the idea of communicating to an audience unnerves you, follow the advice I got from my friend Cindy. When I was starting out in my first career as a radio DJ, she was one of my best mentors. Cindy gave me the friendliest picture of herself and suggested placing it close to the microphone. Whenever I started to get self-conscious or "sound like a DJ," I looked at Cindy's picture and tried to speak as if I was just talking to her. You may discover that it doesn't really matter if you're speaking to an audience of one, or a million. Think about a great friend in your life, like Cindy, and just talk to her.

Tribal Email

Email is the primary method of communicating on your job search, and the easiest way to connect with your tribe. Personal emails are best if they're short and to the point. Be real and keep it brief. Be timely. Be responsive. No ghosting.

There's something very strange about the way people communicate when looking for work. I don't know why a robotic, boring writer possesses our souls when we reach out to people for a job. If there's one thing you take away from this whole damn book, please make sure that you're always speaking and writing in your actual voice no matter what method of communication you're choosing. Please be *you*. Avoid typos, don't waste time with emojis, and don't let the colleagues and friends you're reaching out to worry that you've been taken hostage by a bad ghostwriter.

Email people you like and trust to let them know that you're building a tribe of folks who are supporting each other by pooling their resources and networks to find open jobs. Don't say you're *thinking* about doing this. Tell them you are doing it.

I don't advise it, but if you decide to just send out a mass email, please don't commit the sin of making all the names and email addresses visible in the "to" section of your message. This is a very bad move for a lot of reasons. You're invading the privacy of a lot of people who do not want their email address shared with others they don't know. There is a reason God created the bcc option.

If you want to go high-tech with this, there are dozens of email management platforms that can streamline the process, track responses, and manage dead email addresses. Some of these options offer monthly and yearly subscription-based services; other platforms are absolutely free.

Tribal Zoom

At the start of COVID-19 quarantining in early 2020, our collective idea of a "Saturday night" quickly lost its meaning . . . and many of our favorite possibilities for fun. Days and nights blended together into a new time called Every Day. Socializing suffered until brave souls decided to start meeting virtually, by video. At first there was resistance. (Wait, you mean I have to get out of my pajamas? I haven't had a haircut in months. Hell, I hardly brush it!) But soon Zoom became a widely accepted way to meet and socialize.

Before the global pandemic, I knew a handful of people that were using Zoom. Then, months into the crisis, this platform became the world's "new normal" and one of the most popular ways to connect with family, friends, and business. Other video providers allow you to engage professionally from the comfort of your own

home. Google, Skype, Microsoft, and more all give you free access to meet anywhere in the world, live on video.

I jumped on to the web at the start of the lockdown in 2020 to purchase a three-word URL for a new weekly series called *Saturday Night Zoom*. I've hosted inspiring conversations with pros in our tribe who've been #iBJA (in between jobs, again), and raised the level of fun to include talented special guests who have all achieved great success in their careers. Stars of stage and screen share their stories to help fuel all of us to keep going and find our own path, regardless of how many hard times and struggles get in the way. (You can see all the episodes on SaturdayNightZoom.com.)

Zoom is a free and simple way for you to build your own professional tribe, and keep the people you care about more connected and engaged with helping you find the working connections and job opportunities you need. Here are some of our friendly rules to make your tribal zooming smooth and effective:

- One team leader vs. a free-for-all.

- One main topic to keep it focused.

- One-hour time frame.

- Set all the ground rules before you start.

- Everyone stays muted until it's your turn to take the mic.

- "Audio only" is fine if people don't want to be on camera.

- Ask people's permission before you share their contact info on the invite emails.

- Invite tribe members to sign up in advance.

- Solicit questions from registered attendees in advance.

- Be willing to share and post the link after the live event for on-demand replays.

- Offer optional email sharing for all the attendees to connect.

- Provide chat rooms as a gateway for attendees to ask questions or offer comments.

- Remind everyone the event will be monitored throughout, and the host reserves the right to mute or kick offending guests off the island.

- Don't hog the spotlight; keep it tight.

Tribal Gatherings

When you're not confined to digital networking only, tribal gatherings are the best way to meet businesspeople in a social setting. Bar nights, house parties, meetups, hikes, weekend retreats, workshops, and industry events all give you endless opportunities to form real connections with people you may want to be working with next. Whether hosting or attending, watch your

spending. Business socializing can become a key component of your job search, but make sure you're not blowing too much money. Make smart investments to see the people you need to meet, and create tax-deductible expenses by networking wisely.

Industry events, conferences, seminars, professional courses, and lectures are all important opportunities to gather with the widest circles of professionals in the tribe. Every big gathering you attend (in the flesh or online) is a new chance to meet more people who may want to join your smaller circle of job seekers. And of course, the one person who can be the catalyst to change your career may be attending one of these meetings.

Budget. Do all you can to find ways to get the lowest priced access to the largest number of professional gatherings in your field. Write off the expense and start meeting more people.

Many online groups offer free access to grow your professional network. Take time to do the research about the right tribes that have already formed in your line of work and sign up for regular updates and emails that bring you the right, targeted job openings.

Tribal Calls

Although this book was not written in the 1980s, I strongly recommend the healing powers of the ancient art of phone calling. When your fingers just can't hammer out one more text or email, and you need a break from setting up the look and lighting for another video, go old school and dial friends who love you enough to know that a spontaneous phone call is an act of goodness and not the behavior of an insane person.

Continuing Education

Depending on your budget, this may be the best time to advance your skill sets and expand your network of colleagues by taking courses that align well with your new North Star. If you continue to see job descriptions that look exactly like the positions you want, but you're falling short of specific requirements for certifications that you don't have, then do the research necessary to take only the courses that will give you the most benefit to level up to the jobs that are currently just out of reach.

Meaning

After experiencing the hardest, most challenging years of our lifetime, affecting our careers, our health, our communities, and our planet, we're living in a moment when many of us have decided to reevaluate how we spend our time and what we do for a living. Many people who survived great loss have begun a powerful search for more meaningful work. That's why my tribe came together. It's no longer just about money and job title for the people I've met looking for work; it's about finding souls who share the need for more sincerity and authenticity in what they're doing eight to twelve hours a day to earn a living.

I believe we all share the same soul, but no two of us are in the same moment or on the exact same step on the path to what's next. We are all individual seekers heading to a North Star. You may not find a million like-minded pros to join your job search tribe, but the closer you get to finding more people looking for meaningful work, the happier you're going to be in your next, best job.

It's impossible to assume that every future member of your tribe is surfing on a social media platform at this very second. But I'm going to whip out my crystal ball and let you know that most of them are riding a wave right now. Let's dive in to find some.

CHAPTER 7

Social Voodoo

Social media is powerful, free voodoo, if you use it strategically and consistently to build your professional brand and position yourself for your next job. Your priceless digital real estate has the potential to be visited by hundreds of millions of people. More readers can see one of your social posts than all people currently reading your biggest hometown newspaper. More eyes can see one video you upload than all the fans of the most popular television shows on tonight. Your next podcast can reach more ears than everyone listening to the highest rated radio station in your city.

You could spend millions of marketing dollars to find these audiences using print, radio, or TV. Now, the equivalent of millions of free ad dollars is yours if you learn to successfully communicate, sell, and stay on message with your professional brand—every day—on social media.

If you waste as much valuable time on social feeds as most of us, you're losing jobs to people who know how to regularly boost their relevance and visibility by creating posts that don't suck. The addictive, all-consuming nature of social media makes it the easiest, most mind-numbing procrastination drug of all time. But this is the moment to drop as much of your personal posting as possible. A dramatic shift to the professional "you" is easy if you commit to using our social voodoo strategies to get hired faster.

This chapter gives you the power to develop and deploy a more authentic, professional voice, customized on different social platforms. Finding the right tone and the daily discipline to activate social media channels allows you to show your value to potential new business partners without ever sounding like you're selling.

You significantly increase your hire-ability by staying relevant in the minds of the people you need to reach. Post content that resonates with the hiring manager's needs and you can develop social media superpowers without spending a dollar. Strength and confidence build as soon as you start using these new digital muscles on a daily basis. Results are immediate. Increasing audience numbers do not lie. It becomes easy to judge how well you're doing by quickly adjusting tactics and developing an effective professional voice to add followers on each social platform you decide to use.

Social media skeptics argue that every app on your phone can feel like a nonstop firehose of noise. Others bring a bucketful of legitimate concerns about privacy to this conversation. If you're hesitant to adopt some of the social media strategies we recommend, I'm challenging you to read on.

Cold Turkey

Shift your focus and refrain from frivolous personal posts you may have made in the past to start building a more productive, professional persona. Every social media outlet you use should have one primary purpose: to boost your visibility and impact to get hired now. The minute you decide to go cold turkey—without posting one more picture of food on a plate—you're closer to getting your next, best job (unless you're in the food industry, in which case, have at it). You may be enjoying unexpected time off, but you're going to have more money for future vacations if you substitute that next photo of a perfect sunset with a post specifically tied to your line of work.

Smart use of social media gives you priceless free access to the person holding your next paycheck. The hiring manager you want to reach may be protected by an assistant, human resources reps, or internal recruiters. These gatekeepers make it harder for you to get direct access. You can be forced to wait weeks or months to get near the real boss for a first interview. That top dawg is more likely to be on social media right now, than not. All you need to do is find each other.

#OhMyGod, It's the Future

Not long after Twitter was launched, I was in my office late one night trying to figure out how to suck less at using their new platform. A smarter social media mastermind on my team had just given me a Twitter lesson earlier that day. Her teachings were full of knowledge that felt scary at first. But it was obvious she was speaking a new language I had to learn quickly.

By 10:00 p.m., I was still staring at my screen reading tweets and trying to figure out if I had anything to add to this worldwide stream of consciousness. Could I write anything compelling enough to grow my business?

At the time, I was a relatively new entrepreneur, running my own digital studio and network called My Damn Channel. One of our earliest original hit series was a uniquely twisted comedy called *You Suck at Photoshop*. Our online video episodes were hosted by an off-camera expert named Donnie Hoyle (voiced by Troy Hitch). Donnie introduced himself in episode one as a master of all the latest techniques of photoshop. But Donnie was more than just a tech wizard. He was also a full-blown wiseass who took pleasure in this series of "mocutorials" by berating every potential photoshop student for being too dumb to learn any of his master tools in every episode. Our fictitious host had a personal life that was unraveling one week at a time. Donnie's wife was cheating on him, and his insane, nasty reactions set his life on a collision course with disaster. *You Suck at Photoshop* was fast becoming an early hit series on YouTube. Every new episode was earning hundreds of thousands of views—some episodes captured millions of views. Major press attention included a full-page story in *Time* magazine. We were winning industry awards and passionate fans all over the world were turning our show into a phenomenon.

The social media moment that changed my life (and almost made me a dot-com zillionaire) happened at exactly 10:32 p.m. on that same late night at work. I was gazing at all the tweets flying in at breakneck speed when I received a notification that a new follower had just joined my feed. I gasped when I realized who connected. Another one of my teammates was still in the office with me, seated about twenty feet from my desk. I yelled out, "BRAD!!!!" He came running to see what was wrong. I pointed to the name of the new follower on my Twitter account. I asked Brad, "Is this really him!?"

Brad said, "Oh my God!"

My new follower was the cofounder, inventor, and CEO of YouTube, Chad Hurley, a visionary responsible for changing the future of communication, media, and the minds of most humans on earth. I sent Chad back a direct message (DM), simply writing: "Thanks for the follow."

The next afternoon, a DM came back. Chad wrote: "If you're ever in the SF area, I would love to sit down and chat." I thought about how to respond perfectly for a few minutes. (I'm normally a long-winded idiot.) I knew my message had to be short, calm, *not* desperate and simple. I wrote back with one carefully chosen word: "Deal."

As a first-time digital entrepreneur, I just made a social media connection with one of the most important, influential inventors of all time. I gave myself a personal pep talk, with two commandments:

Be Patient
Don't Blow This

I'd never been too patient with anything this important and desirable in my adult life. But this time I waited for twenty-two days without writing back to try for an in-person meeting with the father of YouTube. I didn't wait to let everyone working at My Damn Channel know that our young company was praised and followed by one of the most powerful people in our business. Chad's interest in what we were creating was validation of our original videos, and priceless rocket fuel for my cofounders, staff, investors (including friends and family), and all our business partners. Chad's message was a huge sign that we were on the right track.

About three weeks after this experience, I got a call from one of our lead investors. He had just left an industry conference in Silicon Valley where he met . . . you know who. I was panicked by the thought that anything less than perfect happened before my first meeting with Chad.

My investor relayed what sounded like a harmless, brief conversation. But I felt the need to make sure. I sent Chad back a note that read:

"Heard u met my 'dad.' Unless you're in NY sooner . . . I'll be in your spot 6/16, 6/17, or 6/18 if u can meet."

From there, we began a series of meetings on both coasts over many months. Chad Hurley was the most chill half-a-billionaire I'd ever met. He invented YouTube with Steve Chen and Jawed Karim. Their idea was powerful enough to change the future of the world. And they changed the future of my business. A few years later,

My Damn Channel received a seven-figure investment by YouTube to create original video series for our platform and theirs.

The moral of this story is that the people who can change the course of *your* career are reading and posting on social media right now. I want to show you how to mark your territory so they can find you.

We Now Return to Your Regularly Scheduled Programming

There's no question we could all have rock-hard, six-pack abs if we commit to a daily schedule of exercise to make that happen. (Note to self.)

Your first step to get social media working for you is to take an oath. Swear that you'll never let a single day of job search go by without making at least one professional, relevant, online post. The best way to build your online audience is by committing to regular, daily posting at the same time each day. Instead of treating social media platforms like the endless stream of disposable content they can be, respect these outlets like expensive television stations of old, running your shows on a consistent schedule. Good social voodoo strategy is regularly scheduled programming, like clockwork. You may not be getting paid for this time yet, but there's no question you're banking good credit. Let me please kick your butt into gear. If you take this more seriously, you're going to get some new serious traction in your job search.

I've worked for more than forty years in television, film, video, radio, and podcasting. Every media outlet that built a successful business with a large following made programming decisions about how to format, present, package, and distribute the content they offer. Most television shows, for example, run in thirty- or sixty-minute time blocks. Most ads are thirty or sixty seconds long. Content makers agreed to these rules long ago. And we've been conditioned to expect consistent formats.

These same practices apply to social media. When you start to build a following, be reliable and consistent with the format, length, and scheduling of what you post.

Practice giving people a steady diet of what they didn't realize they wanted. Don't use social media like an unmanageable toddler, running through everyone's feeds dumping a bunch of junk. Have a strategic approach to what you're posting, when you're posting, and where you're posting. You may be unsteady at first, but you'll master the voodoo in no time.

The moral of this story is that the people who can change the course of *your* career are reading and posting on social media right now. I want to show you how to mark your territory so they can find you.

The Voice

You decided on a new career focus by choosing a North Star in chapter 4. That's your new professional brand and everything you post now needs to be connected to that North Star. If you've chosen a path to work in real estate, all of the content shared online should have obvious ties to that world. Don't let anyone who sees your posts lose the plot by finding out that you're sharing real estate content some of the time with content about your favorite food as well. Stay in one universe with one career focus to build a consistent social voice and following.

The simplest way to stay true to the ideal use of your new social voice is to concentrate on the audience you have to reach. Your new social voice is speaking directly to all potential new collaborators. The most important consumers of your social voodoo are the people who can wind up being your next boss. Imagine you're sitting across the desk from the person signing your new paychecks. The way you hold yourself in any face-to-face meeting with this person should inform the way you show up online; your posts should make the right impression if that person stumbles on to any one of your posts.

You want to be seen sharing consistent, positive contributions online. Demonstrate that you're in step with pressing issues of the business and the industry you target. Be where the action is at any moment and talk about what you can see coming around the corner in your line of work. Concentrate on top business priorities instead of minor topics leaders wouldn't be focused on. The voice you develop will sound somewhat different on each social media platform you decide to use, but there are qualities and attributes that remain consistent when you practice social voodoo. Your posts are:

- **Authentic:** This is at the top of the list. Be true to your professional personality. Be a clear-eyed, *honest* broker of the *truth.*

- **Engaging:** Find ways to post content that *elicits a response.* Take the time to study the topics that are currently getting the most social media traffic in your industry and spend most of your time posting, sharing, replying, and commenting on the content that is driving the conversation. If you think about how many major news stories are covered on any given day by a twenty-four-hour news network, you'll find that only a small handful of topics gets all the attention. The same math is true on social media. The more you engage with content already getting the most attention, the better your chance to gain more followers.

- **Relevant & Recent:** In chapter 4 (Star Point 3), we shared the importance of *relevancy* and *recency.* You can find your next job more quickly when you prove to future employers in your social feed that you have relevant and recent experience. This R & R combo is a key strategy to get more traction if you stay timely and hit the most relevant and recent topics in your field with your own spin. Like daily newspapers of old, social voodoo is all about being here now. Strive to make every post timely. Try to avoid talking about subjects that are no longer fresh for decision makers in your line of work.

- **Inspiring:** When you lose your job, you lose motivation that drives you to accomplish the work in front of you on a daily basis. Find ways to inspire and *motivate* your social media followers every day with content that lifts people up, and they'll come back for more.

- **Predictable:** You wouldn't turn on your favorite country music station and expect to hear jazz. You wouldn't want a favorite rapper to belt out Celine Dion songs (although I'm secretly hoping one of you makes this happen). Don't throw your followers completely off track with an unpredictable voice and tone. Your followers like what they're seeing. Don't switch it up just to "keep things interesting." Give the people what they want.

- **Inclusive:** In 2020, America experienced a nationwide racial reckoning to confront injustice and inequality. A conscious, systematic correction began taking place in every industry to promote and provide more diverse and inclusive hiring practices. No matter what your background and orientation may be, your social voice, heart, and soul benefit from a personal and professional exploration of inclusivity with the content you share online.

- **Apolitical:** Unless you work in politics, you may want to avoid political preaching on social media when you're searching for your next job. You can lose a lot of audience if you blend your professional voice with your political points of view. Proceed with caution.

- **Properly Credited:** Borrowing, reposting, sharing any content that was originally generated by someone else are all standard fare on all social media platforms. But please don't steal and present this as original work. Sharing credit and giving a wider audience to other social media voices you respect will win high marks. Don't poach, no matter how you justify the act.

Turn to the next page for a list of some keywords that can guide your behavior, tone, and style as you develop your new social voice:

BE:	DON'T BE:
Authentic	Sarcastic
Reliable	Mean
Engaging	Petty
Honest	Judgmental
Truthful	Angry
Inclusive	Nasty
Inspiring	Elitist
Professional	Argumentative
Accessible	Boring
Recent	Obvious
Relevant	Hostile
Motivational	Pompous
Positive	Profane
Supportive	Political
Humble	Poaching
Vulnerable	Boastful
Credible	Crass
Energetic	
Fun	
Witty	

Bad Voodoo Kills

You need strategies for when to post, what to post, how to manage these feeds, and most importantly, how to interact with every welcome (and unwelcome) guest who clicks in for a visit.

But before we go any further, heed this warning. Social voodoo can kill. Companies are in a constant state of red alert looking for employees who post anything that can reflect negatively on the business. Innocent early days of social media have been replaced by a vigilant corporate eye on offensive posts from anybody on the payroll. I'll skip the list of obvious errors in judgment. If you have to ask yourself whether a post that you're about to make crosses a dangerous line, don't post it.

Learn all you can about your next company's social media policies before you start typing a single word. Read about the latest examples of people who have been fired for using their own personal posts to spread offensive content. We could spend hours debating whether our culture has become too crass or overly worried about political correctness. That's not this book. I'm here to get you hired. Although there are plenty of positive, calculated risks suggested on these pages, don't ruin your chances of getting and staying employed by offending people on social media.

One last thing: Review *all* your previous posts on every social platform and delete the stuff that feels questionable. Do it now. I know people who've been fired by companies that took major heat for very old posts that their current employees wrote years before they were ever hired. Conjure up all the good social voodoo to get hired and eliminate every problem standing in your way.

Your Best Bets

I want to share the best recommendations for which social media platforms you should use in priority order to support your job search. As of this writing, LinkedIn is the most important partner to help get you hired now. This is the first stop for anyone considering you for a job. And it's the best place to find the people you need to meet. I won't be teaching you my best dance moves on TikTok. And by the time you read this book, there may be more new platforms that can supercharge your professional path. Here's a tour of duty in the places you want to practice social voodoo.

LinkedIn

This is your most valuable destination as a job seeker. You need to spend most of your time engaging here. I recommend at least thirty minutes daily. In chapter 5, we helped you rewrite your entire LinkedIn profile from top to bottom. Now you're ready to flex your new muscles and get in the best shape using this essential platform for connections, research, job listings, branding, promotion, communications, and locking down job interviews.

I'm not going to break down the pros and cons of worthy competitors to LinkedIn such as Monster, Indeed, Glassdoor, CareerBuilder, and more. I encourage you to experiment with other sites. But I caution you not to get stuck spending too much time surfing randomly without narrowing your game plan to the targeted company search we detail in chapter 8. My money is on LinkedIn as your best source of information and connection to the job you want.

CONNECTIONS

Job one is to build up as many new connections on LinkedIn as possible. There's no such thing as too many. Every person who accepts your invitation and every invitation you accept brings you one step closer to meeting the one person who may hire you for your next, best job. In chapter 8, you'll learn about a targeted company search to connect with as many people in the exact industry you've decided to focus on. And connect with as many people who work in the specific companies you decide to target. The LinkedIn search engine gets my highest marks. Enter the company you want and then search for the people who work there. When you hit the button to "connect" with anyone, LinkedIn gives you an option to personalize your invitation. I'll give you two options, depending on your preference:

Option 1: You can simply choose to hit the connect button without writing a note, and then get more personal if and when the connection accepts your invite and links back to you. If you take this approach, then I highly recommend that you send a message back to every single person who becomes a new connection. Thank them for linking and let them know (in your own brief words) that you're asking for "a fifteen-minute intro call in the next two weeks to help answer a few questions I have about a job that I'm applying for at the company."

Option 2: You can choose to put that same brief request above into the original invitation to connect. Use the voodoo you like best. I like option 1 because I've learned that when the other person shows interest on their own, it's easy to take it up a notch with a thank-you and a request.

The purpose of growing as many connections as you can is not to impress anyone with how vast your network looks. Your job is to turn as many of those invites and acceptances into actual direct communication for the mutual benefit of people who can help you land a job and for you to help people make more connections that will benefit their needs. Don't just be a taker on LinkedIn. Be a giver.

RESEARCH

LinkedIn is the most efficient first stop on the information superhighway when you need to learn *who works where.* Your journey to winning a new job moves as fast as it can when you create direct contact with the hiring manager. Why start with human resources, or any other gatekeepers, instead of making the best efforts to get in touch with the most senior person at any company you want to join?

JOBS

If you've never spent a lot of time on LinkedIn, I highly recommend devoting significant hours of your first days out of work getting smart inside the Jobs section on this platform. Find tutorial videos online if needed, but explore all the internal job listing tools at your fingertips. The jobs section of LinkedIn is easy to use. You can teach yourself what you need to know without any stress. Chapter 8 will show you how to build a list of companies you want to target. Then, you can use the "job alert" tool on LinkedIn to get email notifications every time an opening is posted by a company you are targeting.

The Jobs section on LinkedIn includes analytics that show you how many other candidates have applied to the jobs that you want. This data can be sobering. I'd rather you think about the large number of other applicants as further inspiration to use every strategy in this book to get direct connections with the hiring managers and end-run the gatekeepers. Your mission is to make sure you stand out and above other candidates by following the advice in chapters 4 and 5:

- Promote clarity about who you are with a new North Star

- Highlight your superpowers

- Don't sound exactly like all the other robots

POSTING

Any content you share on social media as a job seeker should be shared first on LinkedIn. This is the best place

175

to showcase ideas, information, and expertise to every future employer.

Every post on this platform should be clearly focused on your industry and your exact line of work. The audiences you want to reach are the leadership teams at any company where you're seeking employment. Refer back to the advice earlier in this chapter to post content that is recent and relevant to the most talked about issues concerning your industry. This increases the odds that your posts will be seen by the largest number of people in your field. Posts on the hottest topics of the moment draw engagement. Likes and comments are always more important than the total number of people seeing any single post. Don't miss any opportunities to engage with people who make the first move to connect directly with your content. If someone comments, write back, right away. If someone follows your post as a newcomer, send them a LinkedIn invitation, right away. You should be posting at least once per day on LinkedIn. It only takes a few minutes, I swear. You can switch from creating original posts to sharing the most engaging content other people have already posted about prominent topics, and you can add your take to their point of view.

MESSAGING

Just when you thought one email inbox was creating enough constant distraction in your daily life, you need to check your LinkedIn messages at least once every day during your job search. This is where most of your new connections choose to write to you directly, at first. Once you establish two-way communication, it's easier to switch over to your main email. When someone initiates contact with you, reply back promptly. We're going to address the evil act of ghosting in chapter 8. Ghosting is often necessary if you're avoiding odd creatures on a dating site, but being ghosted is agonizing when people you need to reach professionally will not respond. You can't change everyone's bad behavior, but please don't imitate rudeness. Be a pro who responds quickly, concisely, and in a voice that sounds like the real you.

Notifications

LinkedIn makes it easy to track what kind of daily activity you're getting on the site if you keep your eye on the notifications that will pop up throughout the day.

Groups

If you want to expand your potential reach to find more people and companies in your sectors of prime interest, LinkedIn offers a number of professional groups. Search through what's being offered in your industry and then you can read the About section of any group you want to join. It's free.

Upgrade to Premium?

Most of what you need to accomplish as a job seeker on LinkedIn is free. However, there are excellent optional paid services. Premium subscriptions can provide you with more first-time InMail messages to contact people directly who haven't yet become a new connection. You can also see how many searches you appeared in and how many people have viewed your profile (and who they are). More in-depth information about specific job postings including salary data is offered in premium subscriptions. And finally, the premium options get you additional research insights and access to more learning videos. This choice can be costly and you may not need it. But don't ever be afraid to make any smart investments in your job search, investments that can pay you back by reducing stress and increasing the speed to your next sweet paycheck.

Twitter

If you're tweeting, keep it short. You've got 280 characters to use (as of 2020), but this platform is most effective if you express yourself in the fewest words possible. Start finding and following as many people as you can who are working in companies you may want to join. I'd recommend you create or revise your current Twitter handle to be as simple and close to your actual name as you can get. Every time you're seen on social media is another chance to solidify your name in the mind of someone who holds the keys to your next job. If you're too cute, obtuse, sarcastic, mysterious, political, or strange, you'll miss the mark.

YouTube

This platform changed the world forever in 2005. The inventors and founders of YouTube put the power of sharing video instantly, with the entire world, into all of our hands. All these years later, it's baffling to wonder why so few job seekers create and share video as a prime method of communication. Conjuring up good social voodoo on YouTube and any other video platforms you choose gives you a great advantage to make deeper connections with hiring managers considering you for a job. The content far outweighs any high production values you may not feel that you have the chops to pull off. And the risks are worth the effort if you can teach and train yourself to make short, compelling videos to share on every social media platform you like. Start by studying the badrillion how-to videos on YouTube. You should also constantly include video searches in your research for any company you're targeting and for any executives you may be pursuing for interviews. Watching people present gives you a much better sense of who you're writing to—and hopefully speaking with in interviews. If you decide to use YouTube to post your professional videos, don't stress about view counts. Unless your North Star is to be a famous online influencer or an entertainer or performer, you're not going to be faulted for having a low view count for any video used to position yourself for your next, best job. That said, any way you can manage to become an overnight sensation won't hurt, and YouTube gives us all the ability to make that possible.

Facebook

Some inventions grow so popular they can become victims of their own success. At the time of this writing, Facebook has come under harsh scrutiny for allowing fake news to infect the culture and our politics. The miracle of creating internet connectivity for a majority of humankind is not without its flaws and pitfalls. But Facebook can be beneficial. I highly recommend using it to build a large community of friends willing to help your job search. Personal connections are the ultimate leads for more professional opportunities. Use "the art of asking," mentioned throughout the book, to overcome any fears you may have about letting friends know you're looking for help and contacts in your search.

Instagram

Here's where you can blend in a bit more of your personality with your professional brand. However, a word of warning. Your Instagram may not be one of the first places any recruiters or hiring pros check you out, but this is as good a time as any to remind you again that every dumb thing you've ever posted in the distant past has a possibility of damaging the way you're perceived and judged in the present when you're chasing work. I'm in favor of showing your fun side, your family side, and your lighter side, just rein in anything too off-brand for the kind of businesses you want to join, and don't forget to go back to your first-ever posts and delete anything that's making you cringe.

Time Is Money

If you've only got time to concentrate on one social media platform in your search, put serious daily effort into mastering LinkedIn. Every chance you have to reach one more professional on any social media site will increase your odds at scoring a connection to getting hired. Social media is time well spent as long as you commit to being a business pro, turning off the nonsense, and building these muscles every day without fail.

When you devote a few important minutes to social voodoo in your daily routine, the work gets easier and more efficient. You can find apps that allow you to plan posts in advance. And remember to use the calendarize survival step in chapter 2 and commit to a regular schedule of posts to build your audience and engagement. Any contact you establish with people on social platforms can lead to a direct contact that will change everything for the better.

CHAPTER 8

Your Next, *Best* Job Search

When I started my daily video series in 2018, I was fed up with the amount of slow, lame responses and non-responses to my job search. I was craving common professional courtesy to be able to know where I stood with all of my outreach. You always hear people say that "no is a fine answer," and I agree. The lack of *any* answers from the company you are pursuing is a wrong that I was dedicated to making right. I half-jokingly asked anyone watching the first video I posted about being stuck in between jobs if they were interested in starting a new religion called #JustRespond. But I was deadly serious about learning how to become a ghost killer.

Every company who refuses to respond to your perfectly crafted cover letter, résumé, and job application contributes to a dark cloud looming over your confidence. The absence of any response from potential employers on the road to a new job is inexcusable and drives us all insane. There's an ice-cold chill from being ghosted. And if you're still sending completely cold emails, that chill drops down to a total freeze out.

I need to build a time machine to go back and find the first person who refused to reply to a perfectly written email request for a job interview. I'd let them know they were about to become patient zero in a dark plague that would ruin millions of future careers. I'd use every power of persuasion to convince this original ghost to take a few seconds to respond to that job seeker with the following email:

> Thanks for writing. I'm sorry to let you know that we just offered this position to another candidate. But please keep your eye on our future openings and good luck with your search.

I'd jump back in my time machine and return home with the satisfaction of having changed the world for the better.

If you've suffered more ghosts than you can stand, a short email rejection can feel like winning the lottery. A negative response still beats the deafening sounds of silence when you need your next, best job. I don't want you to waste any more time wondering whether people who aren't responding are "just busy," rude, or suffering from the horrible effects of a Mercury retrograde. If you learn the strategies in this chapter, you'll stop feeling like you're being iced out and start getting more of the positive responses you deserve.

It's time to adopt a targeted job search. You can cure the soul-crushing pain of being ghosted by giving up random search tactics that don't work and scavenger hunts down rabbit holes that lead nowhere. Surfing every job site for hours a day, mindlessly clicking on job postings with the faintest whiff of suitability, is not a plan for success. A search without a targeted strategy can turn you into a dog chasing your own tail.

You start winning increased response rates by manifesting a smarter, focused approach and targeting the right employers—ones actively looking to find someone with your strongest skills. Now that you've chosen a new North Star (chapter 4), rebuilt your résumé and LinkedIn profile (chapter 5), found a tribe to support you (chapter 6), and activated social media to promote you (chapter 7), your next essential step is to start a targeted job search. Don't throw one more random dart at another indiscriminate job board. Aim directly at the right companies with the positions that line up best with your experience.

You also want to target the right person in the company. The amount of people who upload résumés to random job postings, without direct connection to someone in a senior role at that company, can number in the thousands of candidates for a single job. You can walk across the United States of America faster than you'll succeed with this strategy as the primary path to a new job.

All the hurdles you face are easier to leap over when someone you know and trust is connected to the right person on the inside of any company you're racing to join. The first strategy for a targeted search is to hang up your random job surfboard and cut loose with the *Footloose* power of Kevin Bacon.

A search without a targeted strategy can turn you into a dog chasing your own tail.

Kevin once gave a movie interview and said he had "worked with everybody in Hollywood or someone who's worked with them." That quote inspired a popular game known as "The Six Degrees of Kevin Bacon." Players compete with each other to find the shortest link between Bacon and any other actor. The name of the game was a callback to "the six degrees of separation," a premise that states that any two people on the planet are only six or fewer acquaintances apart from knowing one another.

You'll get hired even faster if you concentrate on the idea of "One Degree of Bacon." I've altered the game to solidify this essential strategy in your mind. Do the homework to apply for jobs where you can establish a direct connection to the exact person making the hiring decision. If you can't accomplish this with the information outlined below, you've got to fight to make sure you're never more than one degree of separation away from earning an interview with the one person you'll be working for next. If you feel challenged by this task, fear not. You're about to learn how to get it done.

Targeted Company Research

Build a list of everyone you know with a direct connection to the businesses you're vetting. If you don't find anyone you know who is currently employed there, you might find people who have worked there in the past. Your homework starts with everything you can read about the company online. Take a deep dive into identifying as many current and former employees as you can on

LinkedIn. Send brief emails to every connection you can find. Ask for a simple exchange of emails, or a super brief call, to answer a short list of questions you have about working at the company. You're still going to encounter your fair share of ghosts in this search, but don't let those frustrations push you to skip this step. You need contact with people who work on the inside before you attempt to apply to any open jobs from the outside.

Whether you engage with current or past employees of a business you're pursuing, be prepared with questions in advance. You want to acquire the best sense about the upsides and downsides of working for the company.

- Ask as many questions as possible about the CEO and the strengths and weaknesses of the management team.

- Ask people to describe the company culture and the work/life balance.

- Learn about the state of their business, the competition, and the growth or consolidation happening right now in this industry.

- Are the compensation packages in line with similar roles at competing companies?

- Have employees been receiving the bonuses they were expecting?

- How does their benefits package compare to what you need?

- How much turnover has the company been experiencing in the past few years?

- Are there opportunities for advancement?

- Do they normally promote from within or hire from the outside?

- Ask about how performance reviews are scheduled and handled.

- What's their current policy about working remotely?

- Is there a clear mission? Can the person you're asking state the mission without looking it up? (If employees don't know the company's mission statement perfectly, you've discovered a dangerous fault line.)

Here are a few missions I like:

Tesla: "To accelerate the world's transition to sustainable energy."

LinkedIn: "To connect the world's professionals to make them more productive and successful."

Kickstarter: "To help bring creative projects to life."

Targeted company research is your opportunity to find out as much about any potential new employer as they want to find out about you. Google the business and read all news articles you find from the past three or four years. Read every word on their website. Search YouTube for videos about the company and its leaders. Follow all of their social media accounts and keep a watchful eye on their daily posts.

At the start of the dot-com bubble in 2000, I was poached out of a happy, stable job at VH1 for a new venture. I was lured away by a new business with proprietary technology for a much higher salary, a senior job title, a fancy office, and a promise of stock offers worth megabucks in a pot of gold at the end of their start-up rainbow.

I forgot to stop during all their charming advances to realize that I should have done some homework. Who was running this company? What was the corporate culture? How were employees treated? I was seduced by the pursuit and accepted the job too quickly. The honeymoon period was fine, but it soon became obvious I should have thought twice about taking the job, and eventually the situation ended badly.

Whenever I really needed money, I would inevitably make many mistakes as a job candidate. I've forgotten to do the homework on more than a few former bosses who turned out to be people I would not have wanted to work for. Troubling things about their pasts could have been learned if I had taken the time to check. If you ask around, you quickly learn that a strong reputation (good or bad) has a tendency to stick.

Always, always do your research. If you're going to put in the work to land an interview with a company, you want to make sure it's a company you would want to work for.

Avoiding and Adopting

Looking for a job is a risky business. The search can make you feel sad, mad, fearful, miffed, confused, frustrated, disappointed, depressed, and worse. Most of us get knocked down many times before we win that next job, and the only way to keep going is to believe we eventually *will* win. The strategies I'm sharing throughout this book are intended to help you get to winning sooner rather than later.

Before you begin the search for the right job aligned with your North Star I want to get you primed with advice you won't find in classic job-hunting manuals. By avoiding these pitfalls and adopting these tactics, you'll gain more traction and land your next, best job faster.

The Right Fit

- **Avoid Bad Fits:** Don't apply for jobs that almost fit. You're most likely not going to get hired. Companies want candidates who fit perfectly. I know it's a pain in the ass, but it's true more often than not. You're going to save extremely valuable time avoiding this mistake. And if for some reason you masterfully convince a hiring manager that you are the right person for a job that doesn't suit you, that ill-at-ease feeling won't disappear once you're actually in there.

- **Adopt the Right Fit:** Read every word on the job description and really scrutinize if you are the right fit for the job. You're going to need to check almost every box next to the requirements or most companies won't give you a shot at being interviewed. As long as you haven't rationalized a "yes" to anything on their shopping list (and you swear on a stack of my favorite records that you're being truthful), then you can confidently approach the company and make your best pitch.

Calling in Reinforcements

- **Avoid DIY:** Going solo in your job search doesn't earn you any points. In fact, it leaves you at a disadvantage. Chapter 6 on building your tribe helps you on this journey. Not availing yourself of the wisdom, support, and connections your community can provide is just a dumb move. And don't forgo the opportunity to work with a trusted headhunter or career adviser. The knowledge and expertise these professionals offer are valuable resources that can give you a leg up on the hunt. A do-it-yourself attitude might be admirable when it comes to home repairs, but when it comes to looking for work, flying solo makes the journey longer and harder.

- **Adopt Backup:** Get a headhunter, grow your tribe, increase your circle of friends, romans, and countrywomen and -men to give you all the backup you need on this job search. Bring expert troops with persuasive powers to join your campaign for victory.

Informationals

- **Avoid "Can We Have Coffee?":** Don't go for the largely unsuccessful strategy of pursuing too many general meetings. The longshot "let's have coffee" approach almost never leads to a perfect job. There are two main problems with this move. First, you're not being direct enough with your intention. You're shying away from the real reason you're asking this person out on a professional date. Second, you could have saved this busy soul the time and hassle of having to come out in order to invoke the phrase they hate saying as much as you hate hearing: "I'll definitely keep you in mind for anything that comes up."

- **Adopt Short Calls:** Ask for a twenty-minute call with a very specific purpose. It's so much easier than the worn-out coffee request. "Do you have twenty minutes for a call next Tuesday or Friday, anytime between nine and noon? I want to spend five minutes letting you know what I'm doing now, five minutes to pitch an idea, and ten minutes to hear your feedback." If they agree, make sure you bring valuable content to exchange. Be clear that you're looking for an opportunity to work for them, but commit to offering ideas that can help them instead of just fishing blind.

- **Avoid Brain Drain:** "Can I pick your brain?" If you've gotta ask this over-asked question, please be prepared to give something in return. When asked this question in the past, my answer was always unequivocally "Yes." My answer changed to a "Yes . . . and." Good brains worth picking deserve a clear exchange. And like the coffee move, you're not being as direct as you need to be.

- **Adopt Mind Melds:** Offer to share ideas, content, contacts, projects, and revenue opportunities that will capture the interest of the person you're trying to approach for a job. When the conversation is mutually beneficial, it's more likely that the person will not only say yes, but look forward to it.

The HR Shuffle

- **Avoid Human Resources Exclusivity:** I'm about to get into a lot of trouble with any reader who's had professional experience working in human resources jobs. But remember, you're reading a book by a guy who is incapable of telling a lie. Human resource professionals are lovely humans, but it's not uncommon to get slow responses, generic responses, or no responses from them. Don't depend on HR to get you in the door.

- **Adopt Multiple Access Points:** If HR reps won't respond or get you any direct access to the hiring manager within three weeks, use every connection you can generate from all of your contacts to end-run the gatekeepers and go directly to a decision maker. You'll get over the fear of offending an HR rep who isn't responding if you're able to get to the person who can move your ball on their own.

Cold Emails

- **Avoid Cold Emails:** They're not going to work. The odds are no good. Replace all the time you've been using to send cold emails straight into oblivion with a strategy that identifies warm-blooded humans currently working in companies where you're trying to score an interview.

- **Adopt the Kevin Bacon Approach:** Do everything it takes to find just one degree of separation between you and the person making the hiring decision. The normal six-degrees-of-Kevin-Bacon separation theory is still five degrees too many to win the day. You've got to put in the time like a digital private investigator to keep working all of your best professional connections on LinkedIn, everyone in your contacts, and on any social platforms to get in touch with the one person who can make a direct introduction to the highest ranking exec at the company where you want to work.

Keep Your Eye on the Prize

- **Avoid Next Job, Any Job:** Pressure builds every day you're out of work. Be careful when that pressure pushes you to mindlessly consider taking any job out of panic. If your emotions are clouding your ability to evaluate a job, chances are good that you can lose your focus and make bad decisions. Don't turn a blind eye to red flags warning you that the job is one you should pass on.

- **Adopt a Discerning Eye:** As you research every company on your target list, ask yourself if all of your requirements are being met and if you have any hesitations about what you are learning. Some red flags include:

    ◊ Uncertainty about the boss

    ◊ Role is too junior

    ◊ Company mission is not clear enough

    ◊ Staff is too small

    ◊ Company is too big

    ◊ Salary is too low

    ◊ Commute is too far

Risk

If you've found your North Star, done all your homework, and you know what you want to aim for, then it's time to just go for it. Don't let the "No" Police scare you into inaction. Don't let past failures, fear, or insecurity keep you from your dream. You have to take some risks if you want to get your next, best job. Calculated? Yes. Based on experience? Yes. Based on everything you've got in your head and your gut? Yes. But if you don't take a risk, you're never going to end up doing what you really want to do. Have an A plan. Have a B plan. Have a C plan. But take a risk. You can overthink yourself into oblivion and avoid making *any* decisions, let alone the best decision available given all the facts on hand. The next move your heart, head, and feet need to make will always be accompanied by a level of risk. Sitting still fearing a leap into what's next can become a self-fulfilling prophecy that extends your job search on for far too long.

If your head and heart are telling you this is the right move for you, then you just have to jump all in. Once you decide to put all you've got into winning a role, the worst that could happen is you don't get the job. But you will be more battle-ready for the next opportunity that comes along. And if you follow the strategies in this book, next opportunities *will* come along.

The Straight Line Theory

You may be able to win the true job of your heart by starting at a more junior level than you thought you were willing to consider. I call this the "Straight Line Theory."

The Straight Line Theory gets you closest to your ideal destination in the shortest amount of time. Instead of moving far left, or right, or spending too much time south of where you want to be, the theory is based on the idea that getting a job, any job, that eventually lines up straight with your North Star will keep you on course.

If you want to be a filmmaker, but you're spending countless hours working in an accounting firm to "pay the bills," you'd be best served by quitting that job and finding any role in accounting connected to the film business instead. The rule of proximity gives people closest to the action the best chance of winning more opportunity. Be the right foot in the right door. Don't go for any "entry-level position." Go for an entry-level position in the right industry, in the right type of business, with the right kind of people doing the work you believe that you should be doing.

You'll be in a straight line to move forward in the right direction instead of being hundreds of miles away from what you ultimately want to be doing. You can earn a living and stay on course with your highest intentions if you're doing work as close to the action you want. Don't veer off into roles that have nothing to do with the work you know you're meant to be undertaking.

If you're in the early stage of your working life, before you put your foot into any door, you need to spend some important time thinking about which door you want. Too many people have absolutely no idea what their next job should be. If you're more fortunate, and you've got the inspiration and the ideas of what you want to pursue, then these are ideas you should be acting upon. Say your heart and mind have been holding on to the belief that you have the right stuff to pursue a career in fashion. Then the "No" Police bust through every time you start to imagine how to turn that belief into the right job. The "No" Police will stuff a dream into the backseat and drive you along the safest, most practical path to earn money, even if that path is far away from your ideal job. Stick to the Straight Line Theory and get closer to the job of your dreams.

Luck

I have the good fortune to know a great guy named Danny Goldberg. He leads a creative life working in music and writing, and advocating on issues to defend peace, justice, and freedom. A few years ago, I was at a low point on a really bad day in between jobs. I thought about all the times Danny would spontaneously call and say, "Let's go to lunch." And in an attempt to get myself out of this funk I decided to express a little gratitude beyond my sadness. I wrote Danny a short email saying, "Thanks for being my friend. Thanks for always being there. Thanks for giving a shit." In about two seconds, the phone rang.

Skipping right past hello, Danny said, "What's wrong?" He knew. He saw past "happy gratitude guy" and saw "something's wrong guy." I guess it was that obvious.

I opened up and spilled my heart and told Danny how discouraged I was feeling. He listened patiently and let me share, and then said something so simple that I had a hard time believing it.

In an inspiring career, Danny has worked with Led Zeppelin, Nirvana, Hole, Steve Earle, Bonnie Raitt, the Allman Brothers, Warren Zevon, Stevie Nicks, and countless other visionaries. He's managed the careers of some of the truest people in music.

Danny said, "I need to tell you what I tell my artists. Sometimes, after all the hard work, all the perseverance, and all the energy . . . you just get lucky."

I grew up believing you always had to work extremely hard for everything you got. I didn't think luck had anything to do with it. And if it did, luck never came my way.

Again Danny listened, and then, in the warmest tone, he simply said, "You're wrong."

Now Danny talked and I listened, and his wise words made me realize that I had become too hard on my spirit while stuck out of work. I decided to open up to the possibility of letting a little luck into the equation. And then about two weeks later, for the first time in my life, luck struck. I got two competing job offers in the same week. Perseverance led to luck. And it can happen for you too.

If all your outreach has resulted in dead ends and you're feeling bleak, I implore you to not give up. A little luck may be coming your way soon. If you commit to a targeted company search with the strategies in this chapter, you're going to sharpen your aim and score higher than every random dart-throwing job seeker. Your darts have more power, young Jedi.

It's time to get beyond just a foot in the door. Bring both feet. Bring your heart, your head, the clarity, confidence, and purpose to the next big step. It's the path you've chosen, and like a mental warrior, it's now yours to walk. Take all you've learned and win the access you need to get the right interviews that will land your next, best job.

CHAPTER 9

The Perfect 30-Minute Interview

After experiencing over forty years of interviews as a hiring manager, a candidate, a headhunter, and a career adviser, I'm finally smart enough to know that nothing about the interview ritual is perfect—and neither is the title of this chapter. You are about to get over twenty ideas for a more strategic approach to improving your interviewing skills and maximizing your chances of getting an offer. I wish I could promise these methods will get you hired on the spot, but your number one goal in any first job interview isn't to get hired. You have to convince the person asking the questions that the conversation needs to continue—and score that second interview.

First, let's set the stage and agree on the idea that all first job interviews are supposed to last thirty minutes, max. (I don't know who decided this and why everyone went along with it, but it is what it is.) This unwritten rule of a thirty-minute time limit is so ingrained in our minds that the minute your session ends, you're likely going to look at the clock to see how much longer (and hopefully how much better) it went. If we're stuck inside this accepted norm, we're going to help craft every second of your half-hour command performance to empower you to master this essential stage of the hiring process.

Here come the best practices for dodging traps and obstacles and the best strategies to get from the first interview into the hiring zone.

Maximize the Homework

Your shot at nailing the most successful job interview depends primarily on how much you've prepared in advance. You need to prove that you've done more homework than most candidates by showing up armed with an arsenal of relevant details you'd only get from having done the digging, and offering up insightful observations, critical feedback, incisive questions, and inspired ideas. If you bring this level of depth to the conversation, you'll be able to keep the interview momentum focused on the present and the company's future.

It's taken me decades to learn I was wasting too much time in every first interview on a flawed strategy. I sang too many of my old greatest hits. The more elaborate, compelling stories I told about my past, the less time spent on the current needs of the business and the essence of the new job. Drop the idea of singing full-length versions of every one of your old songs, and listen carefully to the flow of the actual conversation. Then, whip out a few hits, and only if they relate perfectly to questions you're asked. And be ready to sing just the most important part of that song.

You've got to prove that you've put in the time to understand the guts of what the business is doing.

Repeatedly turn the focus of your answers back to what's now and next for their business. Answer every question about one of your past jobs as clearly and succinctly as you can. And connect the answers to the homework you've done by using present-day examples of what's going on inside their company.

Back in the day, I was in between jobs when I got a call for an interview that would eventually lead to a twelve-year run at MTV and VH1. At the time, I was close to broke, living in a tiny apartment with no frills, no TV, and no cable. But I had a friend who had these luxuries, and I knew I had to do my homework. I called Russ and told him that I was going to need to move in for at least three days to study up for what could be the coolest job ever. I took my spot in front of that magic screen and wrote down everything I saw and heard on MTV for three days straight. (Thank you, Russ.)

I flew across the country to NYC for the interview, lugging pages and pages of notes along with me into the room. I was wearing a ridiculous blue suit and tie, and shiny new black shoes. My notes had comments on every minute of every hour of every day covering all that MTV was saying and playing during those three days—all the music videos, the VJ segments, the commercials, the news breaks, the promos. The open job was manager of music programming, one of the very few people responsible for deciding what the world would see and hear from MTV. Every element that made up the twenty-four-hour schedule had to be set up by that manager and their team in a marriage of massive logistics, creativity, coordination, and data.

The person who shows up for a job interview like this has to come in with a lot more than a few stories about past success. You've got to prove that you've put in the time to understand the guts of what the business is doing.

In today's job market, there are too many candidates like you trying to get from the unemployment line to the front of the line for consideration to get hired.

Study. You can't do too much prep for a job interview. The more work you do in advance, the better first impression you'll make. It's easier to talk about what matters to them and not just prattle on about yourself. (Track back to chapter 8 for a detailed hit list of the research and homework you can do before any first job interview.)

Rehearse, Rehearse, Rehearse

Don't go into any interview cold. Get fully warmed up first by running through one or more full rehearsals with someone you trust. Even when you feel highly confident, getting rock solid in rehearsal is the best way to increase your chance to stick the landing. Phone a friend and ask for at least an hour to run through a dress rehearsal for every job interview. (Your real friends will be happy to volunteer.) Set up rehearsal at least one day in advance of the actual job interview. Don't leave this for game day. Send your rehearsal friend an email with as many potential questions you can think of for the mock interview well in advance of your time together.

Include your best short answers for every question. This lets your prepper help you stay on point.

Look Sharp

Your decisions about clothing should match your best definition of business casual. Google it if you're not sure. Choose the look that makes you feel your finest without going over the top. There's advice that says that you can't overdress for an interview, but I beg to differ. As long as you're able to present a solid professional appearance, there's an important upside to feeling reachable and approachable. Ask the people who love you to let you know if the way you're planning to present yourself in the job interview is on the money or off the mark. Look great and feel good. The more you wear a natural smile, the better. If a smile isn't coming naturally, try imagining that you'll never have to interview for another job again.

Make a True Connection

Your mother was right when she told you to "sit up straight!" Good posture telegraphs confidence, competence, and ease. The most important thing to remember about your posture during an interview is to sit straight up in the chair with your feet flat on the ground (never crossed), and hands in your lap. Sit strong and confident. Project comfort and focus. Please, please don't fidget.

Keeping great eye contact is essential for establishing rapport. But here's a secret that I learned long ago. Don't look directly into the person's eyes. Set your gaze upon the interviewer's third eye, just above the central point of the eyebrows. Find this and focus there. It won't seem like you're doing it. It won't be weird. The interviewer won't think you're staring at their forehead, they'll feel like you're making a great direct connection. Your gaze on this spot helps form a deeper bond on a higher plane of consciousness. Ideas about this region aren't merely the realm of mystic sages, psychics, sixth chakra devotees, or Cyclops. Your third eye provides access to intuition. Following this simple technique creates calm for you and the person asking the questions, so you can make a true connection.

Stay Present

One of the benefits of owning the tightest, best new rewrites of your LinkedIn and résumé (chapter 5) is to ensure that most of the questions that would normally come up about your responsibilities and accomplishments in past jobs are clearly understood in advance (assuming the interviewer took that precious thirty seconds to read your damn materials). Presenting all the best evidence about your past success on the résumé before an interview maximizes your ability to save time and stay focused on the present during the actual meeting. Give the interviewer every opportunity to see, hear, think, and feel what it would be like to have you working with them right now. Make the most convincing case by bringing the ideas, experience, attitude, positivity, passion, confidence, maturity, and respect. Be present in your interview. Be in the here and now.

Give examples of the actionable value you'd bring to their top priorities, and they'll want to set up a second conversation to hear more specifics about what you would deliver. You can also drop a few Jedi mind tricks during a first interview to help increase the odds of getting called back. "Here's a short answer, but I'd love to talk about this in more detail in a longer conversation."

KISS

For god's sake, please "Keep It Simple Stupid." The shortest answers during a thirty-minute job interview create the maximum number of topics you can cover together.

Dear Person Who, Like Me, Always Forgets
    to Give Short Answers:

I'm the type who likes to talk—a lot. My best friends still love me anyway. But being long-winded is not ideal in a job interview. (It's not too good on the job, either.) I used to have a bad habit whenever I was pitching for anything that required approval. I'd repeat my main selling points more than once, sometimes more than twice (this reveal is getting embarrassing now). The best practice is say what you need to—succinctly—and then wait for the other person to respond. It took me too long to understand the waiting isn't the hardest part. The waiting is the best part once you're actually in the middle of a job interview.

Patience is a great skill. If you're not over-sharing or rushing, you'll be more confident and you'll definitely appear to be more present when you wait for each response. Give it a beat before you speak. And then tailor your next answer to where the interviewer wants you to go. In the first interview, showing you can listen is as important as demonstrating how well you can speak.

As a child, I was hardwired to think that getting a yes from my parents was no easy task. I must have been so afraid of not getting what I wanted that the potential pain of rejection trained me to use all powers of persuasion—repeatedly—to get the best shot at not being turned down. That tactic yielded one of two results. Either my parents would cave and give in because they just wanted to shut me up, or they'd get angry and send me to my room. Neither response is one you want to elicit from your interviewer. Rein it in.

Plus, do the math. There's no time to give more than one answer to each question in the perfect job interview. Think about your thirty minutes like an athlete. Score as many points on separate shots as possible. And here's a trick: Imagine that the person running the interview wants you to score and win. Try not to see them as your opponent. See the interviewer like your own quarterback, constantly throwing passes they want you to catch. But remember, if you take ten minutes to run all over the field with the first ball caught, you've wasted one-third of the entire time on the clock.

Short answers are essential. Practice.

> Love & "KISS"
> Rob

Be You

If you're trying to be someone you're not, you're probably not going to get this job. Stick with a better strategy. *Be You*. Put your real face on. Don't try to be someone you think they want you to be. In the end, if you do win this job, the masks will eventually come off and they learn more about who you really are anyway. Go all in on honesty, trust, and transparency. If it doesn't work out in the interview, that's because the person on the other side of the table was not the right person you should be working for.

Stay Alive

Be willing to go off script from your well-rehearsed game plan. Don't be a slave to what you thought the running order of questions would be. If you've worked out the best playbook for how you want the conversation to go, and you've anticipated most of the questions in advance, be ready to pivot to any topic at any time. If you come off sounding too prepared and too rehearsed, you won't sound natural. And be brave enough to throw out the game plan if the meeting goes in another direction. This is an important reason why getting a friend to rehearse with you before every interview really counts. It's a priceless chance to work out the kinks, the stutters, delays, and those two-second, buzz-killing blank stares. Ask your prepper to push and inspire you to "stay alive" by fielding oddball questions like a super pro.

Score Honest Points

Picture a huge yellow caution sign when you hear any incoming questions about a specific experience that you know you don't have. Your nervous instinct may be to push back with the confidence that you have enough "transferable skills" to make an easy pivot. Resist the impulse to whip out an answer that will not succeed: "I'm a very fast learner." Please avoid this trap. No matter how convincing you want to turn a no into a yes, you lose big points if you blow this moment. You gain points with an honest, direct exchange like this:

Q: Have you ever managed a large team?

A: No. But in my last position, the organization supported me with one supervisor, one assistant, and an intern.

In every perfect performance, your answers should always be direct, promote trustworthiness, and refrain from any attempts to fake your way into telling the interviewer what they want to hear. Get as close to the experience you're asked about without sounding forced with your answers.

Embrace the Softballs

You're playing minor league softball if your interviewer tosses up recycled antique questions like: "What are your strengths and weaknesses?" I'll stop boring you with baseball analogies and grab my tennis racket. If the interviewer simply asks you to share strengths and weaknesses, take that easy lob over the net and smash it back hard with a unique spin to win more points. Instead of singing your own praises here, let the interviewer know what other people have said, pro and con. Don't duck the weakness question, however weak the question itself may be. It's essential to be transparent about how you've learned to make improvements on your path (the kind of insights you gained from working chapter 3, for example). The upside is much greater than your fear about admitting anything that makes you less than perfect.

Grade Yourself

Expect questions about how past managers would describe and grade you as an employee. If you've been in a management position, questions will also come about how your employees graded you as their supervisor. It's important to show as much self-awareness and growth as you can. This approach by an interviewer is richer and more interesting than the simple "strengths and weaknesses" routine. Sharing what former bosses, teammates, and staff think about your past gives the interviewer a good preview of what they hope to hear if you become a finalist, when they move into the reference-checking stage before making an offer. You need to make sure that the thirty-minute interview includes opportunities for you to show that you can handle anything thrown your way. In addition, if you're talking about a potential management position, it's essential that you emphasize your ability to delegate, give clear direction, reward success, and handle lack of performance by your staff.

A hiring manager once asked me a question in an interview that I'd never heard before, or since. She asked how I liked to be managed. It was a welcome twist on the standard job interview approach, and a warmer than usual opportunity to start establishing the rapport you need with the person who may hold the keys to your future. Whether it's during the interview or while you're on the job, we're always managing and being managed— the more thought you give to these issues offline, the happier you, and your future employer, will be.

Predict the Future

One of the oldest, lamest, relics in the game is, "Where do you see yourself in five years?" It's a lazy question. But here's the good news: If they throw you this soft-ball, picture yourself in the World Series, in the bottom of the ninth, with two outs and three players on base. It's grand slam time, my friend. Take this slowest pitch of all time and skyrocket into the job interview hall of fame with an original answer. This can be a fun part of your rehearsals if you prepare for this moment by adding the personality and humor missing from the "five years" question.

For example: Five years from now, I'd like to be on the top five list of employees who always gave you the most fun answer to this question . . . I'd like to be on the top five list of your best hires . . . I want to get you results that are five times better than you expected . . . and I want to help get you five times more successful by working my ass off.

Play Your Greatest Hits

In chapters 4 and 5, you did the work to hone in on your greatest hits on your new LinkedIn and résumé profiles. Now it's time to take those hits out on the road and sing them live during the interviews. Remember to keep these suckers short. You want to use elevator pitch versions of your best achievements and avoid spinning any long tales. The interviewer may make it easy by going with a general approach like, "What's the one thing you're most proud of in your career?" Or, you may be asked to run through some of the individual jobs in your journey and hit the highlights from each of your past roles.

When you share stories about claiming credit, make sure to find ways to share the spotlight with teammates, managers, and staff. Let the interviewer know how past successes helped make the company a more positive working environment, and be specific about how the end result impacted the growth of the business.

Your best short stories need to be well rehearsed in advance so they don't sound like the same old song and dance you always use in interviews. Freshly shape every story to be most relevant to this company's mission. Examples you decide to use don't all have to be massive hits. It's more important that they come off as natural reactions to the actual conversation happening in the moment. And again, remember to use examples that are most recent and most relevant to the business at hand.

Handle the Conflicts

Interviewers often ask about problems in past jobs. Don't sweat these questions. See them as an opportunity to show your ability to handle difficult situations. You may be asked to talk about how you responded to adversity in previous jobs. Be very careful with this topic. On the one hand, you should never bad mouth anyone you worked for, or people who worked with or for you in the past. But you do want to show your next boss how you dealt with challenging people and projects. (See chapter 3.) You need to rehearse how to briefly talk about any past conflicts. Let people know how you faced and resolved issues without throwing anyone under the bus.

Some interviewers will ask you to talk directly about a time when you had to fire someone. This is an opportunity to show that your management experience has been firm, fair, and free of mistakes that could land your new employer in a lawsuit should any trouble surround a future termination.

The toughest questions to answer come if asked about a time you were given a warning, either by your boss or by someone in the HR department. Tread carefully, my friend. You're going to need to tell the truth, because this topic can be discoverable if they decide to dig. Keep it short. Keep it real. And let the interviewer know you took responsibility and learned how to avoid this in the future.

Tame the Elephant

If the "No" Police are lurking in your head before a first interview, they may be bringing up one or more of your top worries—worries about why you could be passed over for another candidate in this race. In my last few times in #iBJA (in between jobs, again), I was worried that I'd be seen as overqualified for the position. Previous job titles that were higher on the totem pole than the job I was pursuing could be the big fat elephant in the room.

After too many failed attempts trying to figure out how to best deal with this elephant, I finally decided to never let a first interview go too far without leading this gentle giant out into the room and taming it, like a pro, before it became an issue. Tame the elephant in the room by letting your interviewer know what your intentions and motivations are for wanting this job at this point in your career. I let the interviewer know, for example, that I had no issue with a more junior title because the responsibilities and opportunity to work for the right manager at the right company were much more important to me. The truth is your friend in all instances, especially here.

Your "elephant" could be an assumption about the location of the job requiring a move on your part. Although this topic normally comes up during the vetting process before an interview, you need to let the company know that you're fully aware of the reality that the job requires a move, and that you're willing to work with them to make that happen. Ask your "preppers" to help work on your full list of elephants, and turn all that fear of being crushed into the surprising highlight of your thirty-minute circus act to win a second interview.

Be Ready to Hit Curveballs

Here's a hearty welcome to all of the Monty Python fans in the house: "NO-body expects the Spanish Inquisition!" Wise final preparation for perfect interviews should step way outside the box. Brainstorm as many unusual questions as you can imagine. Once you get to the bottom of the ninth, or potentially anywhere during the game, the smartest, most experienced pitchers will throw curveballs to see how fast you can answer their favorite tough questions that "NO-body expects." One part of me hates this approach by an interviewer. It usually strikes me as being too strange and playful for the serious business on the table. But let's give the curve ballers the benefit of the doubt and embrace their odd questions for what they are—an opportunity to lighten the mood. Let's be real: Who really cares what kind of a tree or an animal you would be? These questions are just annoying. But a curveball doesn't have to be something as silly as that. You should rehearse for sudden questions that are designed to get you thinking fast and hitting a harder pitch like: "What's the one thing that makes you the strongest candidate for this job?" If you get a game-winning moment like this, grab the opportunity to reinforce the number one selling point that you should have already hit at least two or three times in the conversation. Focus is your friend in this entire process. You shouldn't have a ton of reasons why you're the best candidate. Try to narrow that list to one or two selling points you should repeat.

Know Your Type

Many companies use personality assessments to know what kind of psychological profile their potential employees would bring to the team. Even Ray Dalio [*Principles* assessments] and the CIA rely on personality tests. The Myers-Briggs personality assessment is one of the most popular management tools around. It brings more substance, logic, and analysis to the lifelong experience of learning how to get along with all different types of people in the workplace. If you don't know what an ENFJ means, this is a good time to read up on the Myers-Briggs sixteen different types. Whether it's Myers-Briggs, numerology, or Jungian archetypes, these assessments give workers and employers more tools to appreciate the value in different strengths, weaknesses, and preferences that affect the way we all communicate on the job. The better you understand how others think, process information, manage stress, and socialize, the more productive the work environment will be. If this question does come up during an interview, you will be way ahead of the candidates who draw a blank stare.

Dream On

Although this may seem like another general interview question, you should carefully prepare the best single answer to this: "What's your dream job?" Your response is going to paint an important picture in the mind of the interviewer about one of their main concerns. A great boss wants to learn about the true aspirations of their employees in order to help them grow and achieve the level of success that's most important to them. A less confident boss is going to use every interview to make sure they're hiring people who won't present a potential threat or outshine their own position on the ladder. When you respond, you want to show aspiration, drive, and a willingness to learn more over all the years it will take to get there. Steer clear of levity here. Your "dream job" answer should stay in the same logical universe as the industry that you're hoping to be hired into now. Tackle this sucker seriously and give the interviewer a sense that you've done the same deep thinking we hope you've already accomplished in chapter 4, finding your North Star. Show that you understand the career steps it's going to take to get where you want to go.

Avoid venturing too far outside the realm of a logical answer. Trying to be wildly interesting and creative with a dream job that's got nothing to do with the present reality of what you may be hired for now wastes an opportunity to show you're focused on the clear path that fits this role.

Work Your Core

A common interview question is, "What's the best advice you've ever been given?" Show growth and self-awareness by sharing an anecdote about how you've been inspired and educated by people you worked for in the past. This is an opportunity to share advice from a previous boss. And rather than overthinking a moment like this, express a core belief that makes you who you are. For example: The best advice I've ever received came from my first boss who told me that I would grow more by doing all I can to solve pressing problems on my own, before elevating it up the chain of command. And he also taught me that it's equally important to overcome the fear of looking bad if there's a real need to bring a critical problem I can't solve to the boss for help before it's too late.

Show Me the Money

You will rarely be asked about salary expectations in a first interview with the hiring manager. The topic will often come up with recruiters and human resource reps who want to make sure that you're in the correct range for the salary they have budgeted. Whenever the question does come up, you want to handle it perfectly. You've likely heard the standard advice that you should never negotiate against yourself. You start the entire process off on the wrong foot if you toss out a number that's too low or too high for the position. This is a rookie mistake you need to avoid. If the interviewer asks what your salary requirements are, let them know that you've done your homework and you're certain that if you get the offer, you'll be able to make an agreement. Your confident answer will surprise most interviewers, in a good way. But you really need to do the homework. Research comparable salaries online and reach out to as many people as you can to find out about the salary range at the company you are pursuing.

Whatever you say, *do not give them a specific number.* Here's how you should navigate: You will likely be asked how much you're making on your current job, or on the last job you held. Lying is not an option. But the best way to field this question is to be ready to answer with the approximate range of your last total compensation package, inclusive of bonus and benefits, to put yourself in the best position for the strongest offer.

If you have evidence that the position you want pays significantly less than your last job, it's essential that you diffuse this bomb from going off. Let the person leading the interview know exactly why you have no issue with their budgeted range of salary for this position. You need to make this case very carefully. For example: "I've decided it's time to make a change from working inside a much larger corporation to a smaller company in order to have more of an ability to impact the business. I realize that requires a smaller salary and I'm completely ready to deliver whatever you need at the budget you've got." Once it becomes clear that you are in consideration as a finalist, or the candidate most likely to receive an offer, there are strategies to negotiate and close the best deal. We'll go into that in the next chapter.

Ask Great Questions

I've interviewed countless candidates who came unprepared for this standard ask that always comes at the end of an interview. "Do you have any questions for me?" This is no time to fold with a response like: "No. I think you've answered all of my questions." Don't waste the opportunity to make a masterful move by asking ordinary or obvious ones. Prepare questions in advance that prove (as you have throughout the entire interview) that you've done more homework than any other candidate. The way you end the first thirty-minute interview has the potential to be the most memorable part of your performance. This is one of your best opportunities to show the interviewer your insight, energy, hunger, and thoughtfulness:

- Ask questions about the management team currently working above and below the person you're meeting. You want to understand the reporting structure. You want to know more about the leaders and their core responsibilities.

- Ask about your target company's biggest priorities for the year ahead.

  ◊ What are the top challenges standing in the way of their success?

  ◊ Who are their key competitors? (Offer your best guesses.)

  ◊ How have they been able to get ahead of the competition in the past year?

- You can usually get a good response if you ask the hiring manager to tell you more about a recent achievement they accomplished. Fine-tune the question to be specific about a project that appeared to be a significant win, and you'll likely get the interviewer feeling good about answering.

- If the role you're going for is replacing someone else, ask about how they may be changing the responsibilities to get better results this time.

- If you are interviewing for a newly created position, let them know that you've studied the job description thoroughly, but it would be very helpful for you to hear what they believe the top three priorities are for the role.

- Finally, your star will shine brighter if you ask questions about recent major work the company has produced, expressing curiosity about the process, the timing, and the interviewer's assessment of the results, pro or con.

Know What's Out of Bounds

You're not supposed to be asked questions about your age, family status, or any subjects that could be discriminatory or break the legal rules about what is acceptable during a job interview. Employers should always want to avoid the appearance of bias. Their typical guiding principle should be: If the question does not directly relate to an assessment of the candidate's qualifications to perform the job, don't ask it. Managers hit rough waters when they request information that's irrelevant to your ability to do the job you are applying for. Demonstrate your savvy on these fronts by avoiding these subjects if they come up: religious or political affiliation, financial status, whether you're an owner or renter, and if you are insured. The Americans with Disabilities Act protects against questions about hospitalization, illness, prescription drug use, addiction, and disabilities.

Women often get asked questions men do not, including topics related to protections under the Family and Medical Leave Act. If asked whether you plan to get married, start a family, have plans for day care, would move if your partner got transferred, or are comfortable being supervised by women or men, you do not have to answer.

Earn Another Interview

Remember that your prime directive in every first interview is to earn a second interview. If you sense your thirty minutes is coming to a close, send clear signals about how a second conversation will give you the opportunity to share more specifics that came up during this first session. Don't wait and wonder whether the interviewer is going to make it obvious that you're going to continue in the process. Let them know you intend to offer more ideas on how to drive the business forward. And don't miss a chance for a happy ending. Let them know directly that regardless of where they are in the process, you're excited about the opportunity for a second conversation as soon as they want. Make sure your final words express real appreciation for the meeting and definite interest in pursuing this further, without an ounce of desperation.

Best Next Steps

It's your call whether or not to take notes during a job interview. There's nothing wrong with this as long as you're able to keep focus on the other person as much as possible. Don't look away too much. I prefer to take massive notes privately, the very second any interview is over, while my memory is freshest.

Your notes help inform the most important next step: the world's best thank-you email. As long as your job interview doesn't take place at the end of a work-day, the thank-you note needs to be sent the same day of the interview, before business hours end. If the interview took place at the end of the day, send the email first thing next morning.

Follow-up notes need to be short. Don't fall back into the same boring traps that make every cover letter, résumé, and LinkedIn sound like they come from a lifeless robot. Include at least one or two of the most important things that came up during the interview. These points should reinforce your main selling points, or fill in anything you may have missed. End by letting the person know you want the job and the opportunity to keep the conversation going as soon as they want.

Don't freak out if an immediate response doesn't hit your inbox. Sadly, replies don't usually come as quickly as we like. If three business days pass without a response, send a "reply all" from your last message that keeps the same thread going with a new note that

225

elevates the idea beyond the lame, "Just checking in."
Here's an example:

> Please let me know if you saw the follow-up note
> below. I'm looking forward to your feedback to keep
> this moving. I'm continuing to pursue other positions
> this week, but you're the top priority and I'll deliver
> on any next steps, including more questions, or a
> written assignment if you want to get a stronger sense
> of how I'd approach the job.

This level of elevation beats the hell out of the normal
sense of sad desperation we're all feeling at our lowest
moment. This kind of message shows that you've got
other options in the mix and at the same time proves
that you're willing to work harder to get to the next step
and a second interview. If you're using all of the strategies to their fullest potential, you'll be prepping and
rehearsing and following up like a super pro for every
additional interview that may come during this process
until you get a job offer.

Be open and positive about as many multiple interviews as a company requires you to take. If you're still
in it, you can win it. For any of you that have never had
the pleasure of interviewing at a "FAANG" company
(Facebook, Amazon, Apple, Netflix, Google), monoliths
like these are infamous for having a long process that
can include up to as many as *ten* interviews. *Stay sane.*
Stay strong.

CHAPTER 10

Close Like a Pro

After you've successfully made it through all the final interviews, you arrive at the next, best step in the journey . . . more waiting. The older I get, the more I stop assuming that just because I want things to go exactly my way, and fast, that every negotiation goes as planned. There are always unknowns out of your control when you're in the running for a job. The best mind readers can't see every possible reason why people on the hiring side delay, throw radical curveballs, change course, hire someone else, or disappear. Even if you've been given every indication that a job offer is on the way, once you complete the final interview, the next move on the chessboard is theirs to make. You've got to wait. The only reason you should make the first move during this waiting period after a final interview (and before an offer) is when you've secured a competing job offer. In that case, you're in a powerful position to carefully use that leverage to your advantage. And we'll talk more about how to do this in a moment.

The waiting period between a final interview and a potential offer may take days or even weeks. Intense overthinking is not the best use of your time. Once you do get an offer there is more work to do. If you followed the strategies to getting hired this far, you're going to repeat a few lessons in preparation for receiving, negotiating, and closing the best deal possible. Say it with me: "Rehearse." Here are your strategies to negotiate the best deal and close like a pro.

Tone

The words and tone of voice you choose when you get a job offer create the essential first impression to let the other side know how the power dynamic may play out in this professional mating ritual. So as an ode to Shakespeare, I now present how to be and not to be.

BE:	DON'T BE:
Smooth	Pissed
Gracious	Impatient
Calm	Uncertain
Respectful	Emotional
Appreciative	Dismissive
Responsive	Offended
Concise	Arrogant
Clear	Aggressive
Patient	Passive
Flexible	Hasty
Positive	Argumentative
Confident	Unclear
Balanced	Repetitious
	Long-winded

Eyes on the Prize

I ask everyone who comes to my company seeking their next, best job to list their top needs. Most of the time, money isn't first on anyone's list. People want the respect, honesty, and opportunity for success they weren't getting in their last job. Most clients are looking for a new boss they can trust. *Integrity* is a prime need.

Job title is no longer on top of the "must-have" list for most candidates. It's important to make the case for why your past experiences justify your qualifications for any position you seek. But many businesses have different hierarchical structures when it comes to job titles. A manager in one workplace can be paid more than a director in another. It's better to understand if the reporting structure of the position is consistent with your most recent responsibilities. If you overshoot and aim for a new job title that's too high compared to your last position, you'll likely be passed over by another candidate with more experience. If you're given a choice to work at one company with a higher salary in a manager's role than a similar job at a company paying less for the more senior title of director, most candidates choose the manager's role.

By the time you're ready to get a job offer, make sure you've completed your homework about the person you'll be working for. Before an offer comes, ask to see the organizational chart in the first or second interview to know exactly where the job fits in with the team. Check your ego to make sure the job you're about to try to win is not "too senior" or "too junior." Eliminate or tame any elephants in the room about whether you're the right fit. And assess your value to determine a bottom line salary below which you can't accept an offer. This is one of the toughest things for many of us to do. When you're #iBJA (in between jobs, again), this is a delicate dance with your needs for income and how much cash you have left in savings. You never want to appear desperate, but you want to make sure you have the best health insurance and an overall financial package that doesn't fall short of your lowest acceptable offer. Key factors determining how much total compensation you can get in any job negotiation include:

- Current industry norms for this position

- Current company strength

- Salary of the last employee in the job (if you're the replacement)

- Your salary history (particularly your most recent)

- Whether you are currently employed or in between jobs

- Whether this is your only prospect, or you have another offer in hand (or close)

- Negotiating for yourself, or through a representative like a headhunter or an attorney

- Any prior relationship with the person making the offer

- How you handle every step of the negotiation

- Your ability to close like a pro

The Power of No

One of the only times I ever turned down a big job for a lot more money than I was making at the time came right at the start of my career. I was working as a rock DJ and the music director for a Boston radio station called WAAF. I'd dropped out of college to pursue this dream after two game-changing conversations with my divorced parents. My mom, the former schoolteacher, said I'd be dead to her if I dropped out of Boston University. My dad, the success-addicted "mad man" from the world of advertising said, "Go!" With regrets and doubts (that never went away) about missing out on the fuller education my parents were providing, my hunger for this dream job won out. I made the first major career decision of my new adult life.

Not long after starting, I was seriously tested by Steve Marx, our fearless leader and the general manager of the radio station. Our job was to rock New England. Steve's job was to turn all that energy and fun into a moneymaking business to sustain us. Steve walked over to my desk one day and shocked me by saying, "You've got what it takes to become a successful salesperson." Steve asked if I would consider a career change from the creative team to the sales side of the business. The account executives who worked at the radio station closed deals with local, regional, and national clients to advertise on our airwaves. These salespeople were the highest paid members of our rock and roll family. Steve said I could make three or four times more than my current salary if I switched over into sales. My first gut reaction was to say no. But I knew better than to dismiss the boss immediately. I let Steve know that sales was never something that occurred to me, but I'd give it some thought. I hid the fact that being "a sales guy" didn't feel right.

I presented the situation to my dad, the man who had said, "Go!" when I asked about dropping out of college. He pushed me to take this new position. The idea of changing my stripes from the wild side to the business side had my father leaping out of his chair with enthusiasm. But every bone in my body knew I was happy where I was, making less. I wanted to stay on the creative path and grow from there. I disappointed my mother and father at that crossroads, but they loved the way it all turned out only a few years later.

Steve respected my decision to turn him down. He never stopped being one of the best managers and mentors to all of us lucky to work with him over the years. Steve knew his job was not just to grow money, but to grow his people. He eventually gave me a major promotion a few years later to lead the programming of the entire radio station. The power of learning to say no at an early stage in my career was an essential lesson in the art of negotiation. However, *no* can also be the most powerful word in a negotiation when you actually do want the role. More on this in a few minutes.

Steve Marx went on to become one of the most inspiring, successful sales experts in media. He founded and led the Center for Sales Strategy, teaching thousands of people how to replace worn-out sales tactics with a more powerful strategy of interactive selling. Steve's book, *Close Like the Pros,* is filled with knowledge to show you how to close the best deals where both sides come out feeling like winners. I highly recommend it. We lost Steve to cancer a few years ago, but his lessons are a living legacy and the inspiration for all the deals I've learned to close in the past forty years.

The Long Game

If you've done the work to know your North Star in chapter 4, and you've followed the hiring strategies to be in the best position to win your next, best job, consider "the short money game" vs. the "the long money game." You can't judge all your future success on the salary you're going to win in your next negotiation. If you take a longer view of your career, you should always be willing to bet on yourself if the role you want next doesn't deliver on all your hopes and dreams for the ultimate job. Once you have clarity about the right industry, the right companies, and the right roles, your career starts moving forward with more certainty. The next salary you win in a negotiation for a job you really want is just the starting point for what you can eventually earn over time. If you meet or exceed expectations, you're positioning yourself for a bonus, a raise, and a promotion. Every significant achievement in your next job increases your value to earn more money in a future role by adding credibility and evidence to your résumé. Over time, the long game wins.

Leverage

Every negotiation is an interconnected puzzle with many movable parts. You learn when to take a risk and when to play it safe to get all the pieces to fall into place. You learn which levers to push and pull and how to give and take. You learn when to make an important strategic move in each negotiation and when to stand absolutely still. Your power moves come only when you can create legitimate leverage to make the strongest deal and be willing to walk away.

I've been closing business deals since 1980. I'm more obsessed about doing homework in my business life than I was back in college. (Mom just sighed in heaven.) You need advanced knowledge about the company you are negotiating with in order to set real expectations for the low and high ends of the financial terms of your deal. You need to gather as much information about the current strengths and challenges of the business and their compensation packages as early in the process as you're able to uncover this. And you don't have to be an international spy to secure that intel. You just need to put in the time and effort to do your research online and identify and interview people in the know. If your salary expectations aren't based on any real evidence before an offer materializes, the potential of wasting everyone's time is great—especially if you learn that the position you're seeking pays much less than you can accept.

———

As you might imagine, the ultimate leverage in a new job negotiation comes if you're currently employed. If you're in a relatively stable situation, an outside offer has to be compelling enough to get you to jump ship. You have the leverage to let the new suitor know that you're unwilling to leave for a lateral move. If you hang tough and hold out for their best offer, the company who just made an initial offer to hire you away from your current job will come back with a stronger package.

Let me take a moment to address anyone who is currently employed and not dying to get out: If you end up deciding to stay in your current job, a competing offer can be used as leverage to get a raise, or a promotion . . . carefully. This is a high-wire act. You'll slip and fall if you don't walk this tightrope just right. Don't attempt to leverage an outside offer until all the details are actually in hand. Once you're offered a real deal to leave your current job for a new company, the specifics of the entire package give you maximum credibility to take that offer to your current boss for a conversation best handled in one of two ways:

1. **You're happy and want to stay put.** You know in your gut that you want to stay, but you can't let a rare moment of leverage slip away without going for a better deal where you are. In this case, tread lightly. When you ask for the meeting with your boss, don't be mysterious. Be completely upfront that you've just been given

an offer by another company, and you want to discuss it.

Right at the start, let your boss know you're happy in your current job and want to be fully transparent about your situation. Depending on your level of comfort, or any confidentiality that may exist with the other company, share as many details as you can about the new opportunity. Remember, in this situation, you've already decided that you want to stay. But you also know you'd be crazy not to prove your value on the outside—and try to improve the compensation package where you are.

Using an offer of more money from the outside to push for a raise or a promotion in your current job can create more tension than you want. The best way to ask for more money at your current gig is to offer to take on more responsibility in exchange for a significant raise.

In this meeting, make your points succinctly. Don't expect an immediate answer. Be willing to let it sit and ask your boss to get back to you within the next day or two. Every outside offer should give you at least a few business days to make a decision. If not, you should always push for that common courtesy. Anything more than three days usually makes the person extending the offer smell trouble. If your current boss comes back to you with an offer for a promotion and more responsibility, you're in the best possible position. Still make sure the salary increase is consistent with a promotion to a larger role. It's not a great idea to get a promotion with a new title and responsibilities, but only a minimal salary increase.

If the boss offers you a salary increase without a promotion, and you know you want to stay, any single-digit percentage increase is a legitimate result with proof that your value is appreciated. You should quickly and happily accept. A double-digit increase is a home run. Finally, if the boss comes back and says your request was heard but can't be granted for any reason, or if you're told "not now" but "hopefully down the road," your only option is to thank them for the consideration and restate your commitment to the current job. Remember, you had already decided to stay.

You've done absolutely nothing wrong by making your case for the increased responsibility and compensation. Once you let that cat out of the bag, a chance to step up in the future at this company will be considered. You don't need to fear that you've created any disloyalty if you handle this process with the clear understanding that you never intended to leave. However, if you find that a year or more goes by without any raise or promotion, make sure your eyes stay wide open to the next opportunity for a new job elsewhere.

2. You've decided to take the best offer.
You're on the Olympic balance beam now. Timing is everything if you find yourself in the enviable position of weighing a competing offer against the opportunity to get your current business to match or beat the new deal. If you're really ready

to leave the job you're in, it's likely that the timing driving the outside company to close your deal will be faster than your current place of work is able to move. Your boss may be surprised when you reveal what's happening with the seriousness and timing about the real possibility of leaving. The first reaction you get may not be supportive. It could be neutral. They could be pissed. Be careful under every circumstance. Let the boss know you hope they consider being able to match or best your new offer. Even if you get a cold response, stay measured and calm. You always want to leave a company on the best possible terms with respect, honor, and enough notice. People talk. Your reputation will suffer if you exit badly.

Be completely honest with the new company that's offered you a job. Remember, you'll only have one to three days to be able to work this balance beam. If your current business is negotiating to keep you with a better deal, let the new company know and promise you won't delay responding in the time that was agreed upon. In this situation, once the counteroffer is in hand, you've got just one shot to go back to the new company and push for their best, final offer.

———

Now back to the bargaining table.

You've got to know what
your lowest base salary can be—
that number below which
you cannot go.

If you enter into a negotiation for a new job without any other prospects, you'll have a tougher time winning the maximum deal possible. But you always have the ability to push and pull on multiple levers of an agreement in the time between knowing they want you and giving your final answer about accepting or rejecting the deal.

Know Your Number

In order to close like a pro, you've got to know what your lowest base salary can be—that number below which you cannot go. When my headhunting firm begins every process to fill a job for a company, we get clarity with the hiring manager about exactly what the available range is for the base salary (and total compensation) for the position. Then, in every first interview with a job candidate, I include a Needs Assessment to help them know their number. This decision is made before getting anywhere near receiving a first offer in their job search.

The best way to determine the answer to what you need to earn in a new job is to start with a complete review of your financials. I know you most likely want to hurry up and get an offer you can agree to now—and put out the flames of discontent that surround you when you're out of work. But to make the most advantageous deal, block out a few important hours to figure out your budget: cash on hand, savings, expenses, debt, and any investments or securities. When you're in a difficult financial situation, losing a job creates stress that lulls us into procrastinating instead of completing this simple financial mission. I know. I've been here too many times. But the only way to reduce these burdens is to summon the strength to separate the "logical, problem-solving you" from the emotional you. This is about math. It's not about the entirety of your identity as a human being.

If you've never been as strong a manager of your own finances as you would like, this is the best time to learn to do better, or ask for help. You'll feel a thousand pounds lighter once you complete this simple mission to get your arms around the full picture of your money situation.

I'm about to bring you into a place called the "Perfect World." You are already in the next, best job. You've got the best boss of your entire life. The person you're working for is someone you hold in the highest regard. They respect you. The whole staff and senior management trust you. They give you all the support and the tools you need, and the room to do your job. When there are unexpected problems, your next boss is fair with inspired solutions to help fix what's wrong and make it right.

How's the perfect world feeling so far?

Let's talk about health care. Your benefits package is the best you've ever wanted, at the lowest cost. You get free spa days. Your vacation, family leave, and personal time is way too generous. The commute is a nonissue. The office environment is suh-weeeeet. (Are you loving this?) There's a great incentive bonus package available as well. There's free lunch. And now, here comes the twist:

> What's the lowest base salary you would accept to
> start this new job?

When you answer that question, you've got your new bottom line. Anything less than that will leave you feeling like you're losing and making the wrong decision. You don't want to put yourself in a new situation where you're waking up every day thinking you're underpaid and undervalued.

The Offer

If you've just gotten a job offer, let's start with congratulations. You've already won. Once you know they want you, relish that inner sense of success and feel the good feels. That energy is magnetic and brings more good your way. You've not only won an offer, you've won leverage. They want you. And now you can make the best possible deal, one that fully values your worth. Realize, their first offer is almost never a final offer. There's room to negotiate. But it's important to combine all these flavors in your stew: be realistic, tough, smart, concise, professional, logical, dispassionate, rational, responsive, clear, likable, trustworthy, respectful, optimistic, patient, focused, and appreciative.

The minute the offer comes, usually by phone, listen closely to every word and take thorough notes. Once the person making the offer stops talking, your first words have to be respectful and appreciative, even if the money sucks. (I'm not kidding. I didn't say appreciation is the only response. I just said to make these your *first* words.)

If the offer is significantly lower than you expected, it's fair and fine to let them know you are surprised at the number and need to give it serious consideration before coming back to them. Don't show annoyance. It's okay to feel it. Please don't show it. Cool is fine. Cold is wrong. A low offer will require you to take a day or two and come back with your most realistic counter. But if they can't get close enough to your lowest acceptable number, you've got to be willing to let them know that without X you don't want to waste any more of their time, and sincerely thank them for asking you to join.

If the offer rocks your world and it's a lot more than you were expecting, don't show those cards either. Be appreciative and respectful and use similar words to a lowball offer, because once you catch your breath, you're going to realize there may be more levers to push and pull for more. Don't gush over a bigger offer than you were expecting. Continue to negotiate up because you've just found someone who wants to make you a happy camper.

Taking It Back

With any job offer, it's important to let the company know that you need a few days to think this through with key people on your team. That team can include your partner and your family. You can always use the word *advisers*, but it often sounds oddly too formal. If you're in an executive opportunity that would normally require a lawyer to review any legal documents, you certainly always want to mention that you need to discuss the offer with your attorney. If the deal is a straight-forward offer without any formal legal language, then invoking an attorney strikes an unnecessary tone. You'll never be prevented from bringing any offer to an adviser you trust as long as you maintain any confidentiality agreement you may have been asked to sign.

It's always helpful to let the person making the offer know that you've got people counseling you on the deal. However, it's often best to negotiate the actual arrangement yourself to establish the rapport you want to build on in a successful relationship moving forward. The exception to that rule is for higher end, executive jobs when it's far more valuable to engage an attorney or a headhunter to negotiate the best deal on your behalf. That's a buffer most senior executives prefer.

The Scales of Justice . . .

Break down each one of the components of every job offer and weigh it on the scales of justice. Think through where you're getting enough of what you need, where it's falling short, and how can you tip the scales in your favor without wrecking the deal. The lighter you can be on your feet, the better this dance will go. Don't step on toes. Don't swing too wildly on that dance floor. Show grace and style out there as you weigh the pros and cons of a deal. Improve your position as much as possible before getting to yes.

Base

The most money you're likely going to ever get on this next job will be determined by the final negotiation for your starting base salary. Once you're employed, the best odds for a substantial next raise won't happen again until you earn a promotion. If you're going to remain in this position for the next few years, you may only achieve yearly raises in small, single-digit percentages (sometimes not at all), depending on the annual results and stability of the business, the marketplace, and the state of the economy overall.

Don't ever negotiate in a vacuum, without enough information to set the right expectation. You're blowing in the wind and just guessing without inside knowledge. In order to achieve the highest base salary you can get before accepting a final offer, you need to have done your homework long ago (by following the guidelines in chapter 8). At the very least, search online and make every effort to talk to people who work there now (or people who are closely connected to current employees).

Any hiring manager will push hard to know the exact amount of your last base salary and total compensation. There is no law that demands you give the answer. But the Law of Rob Barnett commands that you never lie. You're on much firmer ground when you counter any offer you receive with a calculated, reasonable higher number. Here's an example:

- A first offer comes in with a $125,000 base salary.

- Your last job paid a base salary of $150,000.

- You are currently unemployed.

- This is your only offer.

- The economy is down and unemployment levels are high.

- Counter with a 15 percent increase of $18,750 for a $143,750 base.

- If they push back, settle at a 10 percent increase of $12,500 for a $137,500 victory.

- If they push back again, take the $125,000 and push for an incentive bonus.

Bonus

I'm a big fan of asking your next employer for incentive bonuses to boost your overall compensation. You ought to be willing to bet on yourself, and don't expect the company to believe you're worth everything you say only based on past performance. That's only an indication of what you might be able to do for them. But like the ol' jam says, "What have you done for me lately?" You're going to have to prove that you bring real value. She who brings the victories deserves to share in those profits.

Your next base salary could be lower than you had on your last job; however, if you know you're worth more, the best way to negotiate is to show you're willing to prove it over the first year. Try to set up an incentive bonus structure based on performance. Isn't it worth investing in yourself and in the company for at least a year?

Time Off

Work is no fun when you're under the nose of a clock watcher for a boss. You're always in much better shape if you find an environment where the results you deliver are of primary importance and not whether you've delivered those results at 8:00 a.m., noon, after dinner, or early some Saturday morning. Ask about the expectations of real work hours, start times, end times, overtime, and off hours before you start. Make sure you get at least the age-old standard of two full weeks of vacation, somewhere between five and ten sick days, a couple or three of those wild card personal days, and the best family leave policies for when life-changing events occur—for the good or the bad. Beyond this, I don't think you should ever stress too much about time off during a negotiation to start a new job. Your potential cash compensation is so much more important. When I'm the boss, I start to feel odd about a prospective new employee pushing hard for too much time off during a job negotiation. It sends a bad signal.

Severance

This is a big one. You want to find out as much as you possibly can about the difference between the written policy and the actual practice of what the company you may join has been doing about severance in the recent past when people get tossed out. In an ever-increasingly volatile workplace (and of course in any bad economy), layoffs, restructuring, firings, job eliminations, furloughs, salary reductions, and broken agreements are all potential demons that pull the rug out from under all of us. When you're the ultimate boss and the going gets tough, the tough never get going. You don't fire yourself. You do whatever needs to be done. When you're working for someone else, and the bottom falls out suddenly, you need as much protection as you can negotiate.

If you're an employee at will without any formal contract, just a standard deal agreement, you may not even see a single word in there about what happens if you get canned. Most companies have a policy of giving two weeks of severance for every full year served before you're terminated. Realize that if you are terminated for cause, you're completely shit out of luck. You get nada. But if you're fired for reasons beyond your control, and due to changes the company had to make on their own, you are due—and should fight hard for as much severance as you can get. Not just at the moment when you're cut, but up front, before you start, in the initial employment agreement. Getting as much protection as you possibly can is essential.

Winning

The pain and strain of waiting, wishing, hoping, failing, missing, coming up short, getting played, screwed, or cast aside does not feel quite as lovely as winning.

Imagine how you feel when you know that you're wanted, respected, rewarded, trusted, supported, embraced, celebrated, elevated, with promises kept, roadblocks removed, and the green light given.

There's a secret battle happening inside, between the two sides of yourself, during every negotiation for a new job: the winner and the loser. When you keep seeing yourself as the winner, when you keep feeling the way you feel when the world goes right, you're filling up with positive, magnetic energy to make this all come true.

The odds that your negotiation will fail are increased every time you let the fear of losing kill your confidence and strength. You can't win this game if you don't imagine the win before you get out on the field. Both sides are about to score points. The lead is likely to change hands multiple times. The minute the negotiation looks like it's slipping away, fear can sneak back in. You can blow your cool. You can give in to the dark side. Don't let this happen. Take a minute. Steel your spine. Snap out of the "emotional negotiator" position and back into the cool character you've got to be to make the next best move. Your confidence doesn't belong to anyone else. It's in you. There's no external power turning your own confidence on and off. You've got total control over your own source of power, your own sense of self.

When to Walk

Here's one of the wildest movie moments in any negotiation. If you've been through more than a few rounds back and forth, and the numbers and levers you hoped to push and pull are not going your way, and if you're not close enough to the bottom line where you can say yes, there will come a time when you've got to be willing to walk away from the deal and mean it. This is your final move in any negotiation that still has a chance of going your way. But there's no faking this. You can only make this move once. Your words and tone matter. Keep as cool as your favorite action movie goddess or god. Let your negotiating partner know you appreciated every minute of their time and willingness to make a deal that works for both of you. You realize they have reasons they can't match the bottom line you need to accept this offer, and you've decided that you have to pass. If you use this strategy to your best advantage, you're going to feel like an action hero.

The response you're about to get can come in many forms. It's best to prepare in advance for all of them and decide what you're going to say before you make this rock-star move. Here are four possible reactions from their side:

1. Wow. I'm really surprised and disappointed. I wish you well. (End of game, they're bummed.)

2. Are you sure? We really want you here. Let me see if I can go back to my people and do any better. (You nailed it. Now there's one more shot and they'll come back with *more*.

3. I respect your decision. I'm sorry we couldn't make this work and I hope we stay connected. (A pro who took it like a pro.)

4. I think you're making a big mistake. Good luck to you. (Bad vibe. You didn't want to really work for this person.)

In version 1, it's definitely game over. Know that you did the right thing. This job was not going to give you what you needed to say yes. Move on with your dignity secure. You've done nothing wrong.

In version 2, you're a negotiating rock star. You've made the strongest move possible and created the probability that the other side is coming back with a better offer, an offer that you're going to want and need to close.

In version 3, it's still game over, but you've earned a real level of respect from the person who wanted to hire you and that relationship can be revived again in another opportunity down the road.

In version 4, you've just seen the darker side of the person you almost called your boss. You did the right thing. And you dodged a bullet that your intuition knew was there. Good job.

"Mutual, I'm Sure"

The best strategy for closing like a pro is to stay completely focused on the final outcome of the negotiation. Both sides give and get, and both sides find agreement in the middle. If you have the ability to negotiate your next job offer directly with your next boss, you want a great beginning to become the model for a great relationship moving forward. Even if the deal is negotiated by a mutual representative, you and your next boss both know exactly how each of you behaved and negotiated during every step of the process. Convey respect, professionalism, charm, strength, logic, clarity, and camaraderie to forge a winning deal.

CHAPTER 11

We Can Be Heroes

It's 3:00 a.m. The moment to write the last chapter of this book has finally arrived on a cold winter night while I'm awake thinking about how to give you one more first-class ticket to what's next. The eleventh strategy to get hired now took me sixty years to learn. Your flight to the biggest secret in this book is a much quicker trip. And I've got an eternal co-pilot to help land this plane.

David Bowie represents constant evolution and reinvention. Like many of the greatest artists on earth, his eyes were fixed on the stars with his feet on the ground and his hands constantly busy working his craft. Bowie's job was a soul search shared with every hungry heart who wanted a taste.

The challenge to find your next, best job can be a struggle met with constant changes. But change is also an internal force that you can learn to manifest, and even master on behalf of the good. The way you embrace, accept, and master change is the work of a hero. The time you give to help other people struggling with change is the mission of a hero.

After surviving the global pandemic and the radical upending of our worldwide economy, the very nature of how and where we work was redefined by dark, once-in-a-lifetime circumstances that, for a time, felt completely out of control.

The job of finding work became a primary need for more people on this planet than at any other time in our lives. The great sense of isolation was a shared experience for the entire world facing survival together and searching for signs of heroism, no matter how small.

In my darkest moments, I've learned that my fear of failure was a prison I couldn't escape alone. I needed a tribe of jailbreakers to help find the work I was called to do. I needed a new North Star to light the sky, not just for my own benefit, but for people in deeper trouble than me.

You can choose to continue to see the struggles in both your life and work as a battle. Or you can take one giant leap back to 2020 and see that our world was completely changed forever by global suffering inside every human heart. We were all challenged to do good work, take care of our own hearts while taking better care of each other than ever before. We are all in this together, and the time we have is precious.

Life is too short to be lived without taking stock of what you learn from pain with the purpose to put your strengths and gifts to work every day. We can be heroes if we figure out how to do the work that's in our hearts.

We can be heroes if we help more people find their own North Star.

If you opened this book in a state of pain and loss, my greatest wish is that you close it with passion and purpose. I'm writing to you with Bowie blasting in the background. We're alive. Possibilities are endless. And the world at large gets smaller and more interdependent by the second.

Find your North Star. Find your tribe. May your passion and purpose lead you to heroic acts of good work and beautiful rewards. Thanks for coming in.

Give It Away Now

I hope you'll share these strategies for a new job search with more people who need to find the answers. Anytime you can help someone use these strategies, you'll sharpen your own tools to make your next stop in between jobs quicker and less painful.

I also hope you'll use these strategies to make room in your life to help people whose problems are far worse than just the next paycheck. When I lost my last job, I was given the opportunity to volunteer for WhyHunger, an organization devoted to ending hunger and advancing the right to nutritious food around the world. As difficult as my time was without a job, my family still had food on the table and a roof over our heads. Our stress paled in comparison to the suffering of people with no support, no home, and no nutritious food.

I didn't have any money to be able to contribute to a mission like WhyHunger while I was unemployed, but I did have an overabundance of time on my hands and a wealth of experience and contacts to lend help.

I remembered an earlier time in my life, during college, when I lived with my best friend, Mike. Whenever I was getting too full of my twentysomething self, Mike would show a great smirk on his face, raise his right index finger just above his head, and start making perfect circles around and around his head with that index finger. This was Mike's favorite way of letting me know it was time to shut up about my problems and realize the entire world does not revolve around me. We all need a Mike in our tribe.

If you devote one day a week, one hour each day, or even one hour a week to volunteering and serving any organization that helps people in pain, then that time you spend in service to someone else replaces worrying about your own hardships. You can lift up the lives of people longing for an ounce of goodwill. Your heart heals and expands when you lift someone who's fallen.

My grandma Janie was an angel from Liverpool. Another angel born there once sang a warning that karma will "knock you right on the head." Janie's promise to me as a young boy was to believe that I'd know what I needed when the time was right. This journey began without a job, without income, and truthfully without a clue. But the moment I decided to help people who needed what I had without any ask for money in return, the answers became clear and the work and income followed. May instant karma knock you softly in the head and lead you dancing into your next, best job.

Author's Note

Born to Run

Rock and roll has always been my best medicine. Lifelong friends are shocked that it took this many pages to invoke my hero, Bruce Springsteen. Bruce taught me to believe in my dreams and keep driving toward "the promised land." His work ethic, passion, and certainty that quitting is never an option all led me to write this book.

The music I worshipped as a kid helped me figure out who I wanted to be, and super-glued me to the friends and lovers who changed my life and created my family. After studying journalism and writing and editing for my high school and college newspapers, I found a first career as a rock radio program director and an on-air personality at stations in Boston, Dallas, and Los Angeles. A few of the people I got to meet in the radio business had become mothers and fathers of MTV in the 1980s. Thanks to them I learned to turn dreams into reality on a global scale during a dozen lucky years working inside MTV and VH1. Those experiences led to my first start-up company in 2000, and on to more passion projects in film, music, and politics.

I then landed a job back in radio as the president of programming for CBS. The radio business was always my first love, but the industry had become too resistant to change and innovation. I got fired by the infamous Leslie Moonves. Minutes later, in 2006, I launched my own radical idea for a media company called My Damn Channel. We were one of the first online studios and networks to create and distribute original comedy series and music for millions of fans on our own website, on YouTube, and on all social media platforms. For ten years, I learned how to grow and run a business that raised and earned tens of millions of dollars and employed hundreds of visionary creators years before Netflix and Amazon started making their own original series. We even predated the iPhone. Like most start-ups, we sought that magic pot of gold at the end of a rainbow. But that glory was just out of reach. In 2017, I had a brief, but unforgettable, experience in a leadership role at Audible. The audiobook innovator owned by Amazon gave me the opportunity of a lifetime with responsibility for marketing the book by Joe Biden to honor the memory of his late son Beau. *Promise Me, Dad: A Year of Hope, Hardship, and Purpose* became a touchstone that I would return to a few years later, when a family tragedy of our own reminded me what I learned over a series of four months and multiple one-on-one sessions working with President Biden. His life story inspired me to heal pain by finding purpose for a greater good.

Within a year, and not long after I founded my new mission as a headhunter, my younger brother Jeff lost his life to suicide. Jeff was suffering mental illness and years without a job. His death was a shock that was too much for me to handle alone. I had the instinct to start talking about this openly and immediately, believing that the most important thing I could do in that moment of agony was to encourage anybody else in danger to reach out for emergency help.

My next instinct was to find crisis counseling. A great man had the emergency expertise I needed. He referred me to a therapist who has never stopped helping me learn more about healing the tragedy that triggered immeasurable pain. These lessons are what drive me every day to help you find the answers you need to turn pain into a better purpose.

Thank You (falettinme be mice elf agin)

My biggest thanks start with two women: my mom for teaching me to always tell the truth, and Amanda Palmer, for teaching me *The Art of Asking*. I could never have completed this book without a host of patron saints who've given me the constant support to serve you. Amanda and Seth Godin are two visionary thinkers and writers who taught me the importance of giving away all the best that I've learned, for free, every day. My daily videos, our *Next Job, Best Job* Sunday emails, and our jobs site are all free.

I had an A-team who birthed this book. Deepest thanks for every sleep-deprived day and night gifted to me by Lisa Fitzpatrick, the best personal developmental editor this first-time author could have imagined. Rick Richter is the literary agent who must have gotten the call from my mom in the great beyond to find me. Rick explained why this book had to be written and it never would have found its home at Citadel Press without him. There, our team led by editor Denise Silvestro gave us expertise and passionate support to share this book with as many people as we can reach. The team inside Rob Barnett Media has my love and thanks. They're led by another heroic Amanda. Amanda D'Oriano has been by my side every step of the way, making sure our company never missed a beat serving hiring managers and job candidates while I multitasked my head off.

Thank you to every company and to every job seeker trusting us to make work marriages that last. Thanks to my lifelong friends I can't live without, and to every new friend who saw this mission and made it their own.

Finally, to the dreamers, artists, and musicians who create the soundtrack to every one of my daily videos. You remind me of the last words my mom left me to take care of my family and friends and get through the rest of this trip:

Strive for the Good.